Oct Tongue -1
ISBN 978-1-940996-08-0
Each poem © by its respective poet

Authors: Mary E. Weems, John Swain,
Steven B. Smith, Lady [Kathy Smith],
Shelley Chernin, John Burroughs and
Steve Brightman

Cover photo by Steven B. Smith
(agentofchaos.com / walkingthinice.com)

Executive editor: John Burroughs
Book published as Crisis Chronicles #55
1st printing (71 copies), 27 August 2014
2nd printing (19 copies), 5 February 2015
3rd printing (10 copies), 16 October 2016
4th printing (20 copies), 24 October 2017
5th printing (20 copies), 2 March 2019

Crisis Chronicles Press
3431 George Avenue
Parma, Ohio 44134 USA
crisischronicles.com
ccpress.blogspot.com
facebook.com/crisischroniclespress

Contents

Preface   9

Weems   **11**

Swain   **47**

Smith   **83**

Lady   **123**

Chernin   **187**

Burroughs   **223**

Brightman   **261**

Acknowledgments   209

About the Authors   301

Preface

On 28 September 2013 I co-hosted the Cleveland edition of 100 Thousand Poets for Change at Visible Voice Books. While there, I saw a book I never knew existed: *February 03* by Todd Colby, Alex Gildzen, Thurston Moore and Matthew Wascovich, published in 2003 by Cleveland's own (now apparently defunct) Slow Toe Publications. I had to take it home with me.

For that book, the authors had each written a poem a day for the month of February 2003, and I immediately began thinking about how I'd like to try something similar with some of my favorite poet friends during the coming month (October 2013). With less than a day to go before the month began (and before I'd even had a chance to finish reading *February 03*), I began asking folk if they would like to participate. I planned at first to have four authors like the book we were modeling. But I wasn't sure how many of my friends would agree at the last minute or stick with it all month if they did, so I asked too many. Almost all of them said yes and we wound up with eight. Since I had already been thinking of calling the book *Oct Tongue* because of the month and a germane allusion to a German word, I couldn't have been more pleased.

One of the participants had to withdraw before October was finished, however. That's when this book became *Oct Tongue –1*, which can be read as both "volume 1" and "minus 1." A few other changes happened along the way, too. For example, in the process of putting it together I decided to vary from the example of *February 03* and group our poems by poet instead of by date. But the inspiration remains strong, though we ran in some different directions, and I am extremely proud of how *Oct Tongue –1* has come together. Many thanks to *February 03*. Thanks, too, to independent bookstores like Visible Voice, Guide to Kulchur and Mac's Backs in Cleveland for giving prime shelf space to uncommon books like these.

Finally, I offer my deepest respect and gratitude to my collaborators: Mary Weems, John Swain, Steven Smith, Lady K Smith, Shelley Chernin and Steve Brightman. In my best Bob Dylanish croon, "If not for you...."

John Burroughs, editor
Crisis Chronicles Press
24 July 2014

Weems

John challenged us to write one poem each day for the month of October. Once I committed to the project, I pushed myself to write several poems each day because I wanted to make certain to wind up with 31 decent ones. I managed to do so on most days. Instead of my usual way of writing poems, which is to write when I'm inspired, I found myself looking for poems everywhere: when driving on the street, while watching the news and while reflecting upon my own life.

— *Mary Weems*

Aging

the bravest thing a body
can do,
each year a bird
pecking, the end
a period in another sentence.

Mary Weems

Grief

That empty rasp
a body makes
remembering.
An almost face,
glimpse of a hand
resting on its lap.

Haiku

October dons a mask
of leaf and feather—
prepares for a long sleep.

Drones

Interrupt the sky
like mechanical dragonflies
I look twice
recall when jets would speed through our neighborhood
make us run outside in a moment of wonder.
Being safe in a world at war with emotion
takes its toll and the line between keeping out and letting
in looks the same.
This time I worry, everyone under surveillance,
even an infant sleeping in her crib, while the stranger
who hacked her parents' home security system
says her name through their baby monitor.

Mary Weems

Lunch Date

I sit across from a middle aged sister I still call
baby, separated in the same
city by decades of mama,
we decide to cross the line our mother drew in the sand, replace
it with another chance.
Between bites we fill in the blanks of stories she's told us
on different occasions, discover nooks and crannies of lies,
half-truths, we laugh too, remember better times,
promise each other to get together.

Mary Weems

Haiku

In the woods a leaf
held by spider's thread
reaches out its hand.

Wife Beater

The disk jockey is making a joke
about parents and children.
He's rushing to get to the punchline before they cut
to commercial. He says that it's time to put your son out
when he starts taking your wifebeaters. I wait for the canned laughter,
remember: Big-balled-fist, stomach, double over, stumble to knees,
tremble, afraid to look up. Listen.

Rain

It rains because:
Clouds need jobs
World needs a bath
Sky needs something to hold onto
People weep
Bad days need moisture
Weddings need bad luck
Funeral cars need a last minute wash

Leftover

A young girl
carries her still born
in the bottom of a shopping bag
like a forgotten pair of panties

Clothesline

There's a woman
in each bra
cup and color
flesh
tone torso,
bald head after
bald head
straps criss-
crossed to hold
each other up.

Irises

Every morning the same look.
I wash the sleep out,
imagine another story.
I leave the house, spend the day
avoiding eye contact like an amateur telling a lie.
I was born with the wrong eyes. The only pair of brown
in a family of blues and greens.
Took me years to save money
for the operation.
After hours of surgery I had my irises replaced—
now my eyes are green—
but I'm blind.

In the news

Today a bullied boy
turned in his homework. All of his answers correct,
his parents' semi-automatic weapon
a surprise to the middle school math teacher
he killed, the two students he wounded
as if they were characters
in a virtual world
before he turned the gun
on himself, all of his answers
correct.

Mary Weems

Candlelight

Power's out. I remember
what we did as kids—
light the gas stove burners, light
candles, read.

Gin

Clear as water
it carries trouble
destroys bridges
makes "I'm sorry"
a laugh. In Liquor ads
it's love, beauty,
money, power, one drink
after another pitched,
the phone number for help
printed at the bottom
like ice in a glass.

Mary Weems

"Fargo, North Dakota woman will give trick or treaters letters if she thinks they're overweight"

The wicked witch of the west left Kansas and moved to Fargo
in disguise, traded her broom for a tree, turned the tree into paper.
According to the news reporter and a written statement, she
plans this as a way of helping overweight kids.
Kids who already know they're not thin, who, not recognizing
her as a scary witch, will read her letters and refuse
to enjoy the best part of Halloween.

RIP
OG
Smoke

Tag's spray painted
on an abandoned building.
For months I've driven by
this headstone, each time pulls my eye
away from fancy billboards
for liquor,
for breast feeding,
fast food.
What matters is this brother
whose smoke
sits on the wall
waits for someone
to look long enough
to see who he was.

Mary Weems

Summer

Early morning. Hot
July. I water our community garden
throw a rainbow.

Fall

shakes the trees
down for leaves, the evergreens
among them stand quietly,
refusing to pay.

Mary Weems

Haiku 10-19-13

Mid-morning. Four jets
fly across bare-blue sky. White trails
an in-flight Morse code.

Mary Weems

A Leaf

Jumps from a tree—suicide.

Mary Weems

10-21-13

God picks up a dead tree,
plays it like a flute.

Pickup Lines

My husband exits his red
Ford, writes this poem in our driveway.
Something about the way he stands, cocks his head,
lifts one blue-work-pant leg at a time, makes
me want to bend on one knee, ask him to marry me.
I think of the moods of love
in a single day, the way we can be quiet, hold hands.
How he can piss me off, make me want to kiss.

Mary Weems

The Washington Redskins?

A racist mascot reminds
that The People have opted out
of the American Dream, passed the nightmare
down to a new generation, careful to explain
the myth. To make certain their kids know who
they are, who skinned who
and why.

Voice from the past

The sound of the cigarette
commercial reaches me from childhood:
"Call for Phillip Morris,"
bell hop shouts, a pseudonym
for cancer.

Israel

10-25-13, W. 37th & Denison

Who could run over
a 5-year-old black boy
with a van and leave as if they'd
run over a can?

Healthcare

The hospital employee
thought patient was a mannequin.
No one knows how she got there.
Official report:
"That hallway is rarely used."

Haiku

I watch Death's assembly
line roll by.
When will I
be first in line?

Mary Weems

**"They only can shoot my body.
  They cannot shoot my dreams."**

Malala, a lion fighting for education
speaks to a news person.
She is calm, the wound in her head,
scar covered by bright
orange silk.
I know I'm watching grace in a girl, a gift
almost lost on a school bus
in the name of religion.

Mary Weems

Local News

is the entertainment channel.
Dress code color coordinated, everything read
even the mistakes. If it bleeds it leads,
a carryover from print focused on a bottom line
shrinking like silk caught in the rain, all the stories
lopsided, mistaken sound bites, rushing from one
to the next in time for the commercial.

It's repeated every hour, 60 minutes all a person needs
to catch up on an entire world of death,
crime, weather, stray cats and dogs.

Haiku 10-30-13

Orange ladybugs
at my office window—
a flashmob.

Halloween

After seeing Bela Lugosi, a Black and White
Dracula, I was afraid of vampires until I was thirteen.
That year I crawled up in my sister's bunk like usual
and pushed her away from the wall, until she fell
cutting her face, spilling blood, scaring
me brave.
On a cool Fall night like this, I can smell Halloween coming:
Pumpkins, candy corn, candy apples, the acrid smell of smoke
from trash being burned in garbage cans, grown folks rushing
to front doors, pretending to be afraid between laughs,
filling our sacks, heavy at the end of the night. The fun of silly,
sorting, eating, exchanging, costumes in place, holding onto Halloween
with both hands.

Mary Weems

Halloween

After sliding into Trick or Treat and White
Night, I was told down past a thirties bitten
that year crowded up in my sister's comforter with Ed,
and passed her away from flex at the other end,
biting her then, hitting Ricky among
me or so

Or a cool warmth like a lost hand reaches out,
Popping candy, my body aches, the soda spills across
floorboards — I watched D&D at 3am, gown bare naked.
Stone core grin in, looks at each sheep, sucks.
Soon, I look into a flicker of moonlight flit in the sky
rolling softly like crepe, turns breeze, yawn into lattice of
ethereal.

Swain

The muse cannot be demanded, although she requires daily offering. Strange and indecent perhaps to call these glimpses finished. The freedom of poetry lives in its mutability unlike the final death. Please find these humble words then as a little notebook of exercise and devotions.

— *John Swain*

1.

Ocean through the eye
of a crow
on the torn fence
lifting itself
away from barbed wire.

2.

Low the sun held
by the cloud roll.
A field of stones
bed morning
past the tree corridor
trembling in wind
like a chase.
I remember your hands
your lucid skin
drawing every color
out of one river
we swam
between walls of rock
bird shadows painted
like a dreamt mask
our faces empty.

John Swain

3.

An alchemical queen
glanced at a feral cat
under lamplight
the summer
we touched
through portraits.
Like people merging
she played cello
on a dark
small oval rug.
My shirt stayed blue
and I sat for an hour
in a wicker chair.
Mangoes
and oranges
and avocados
remained
in a ceramic bowl
on the table.
I reminisced
about ships
made of tusk bone
and leather.

John Swain

4.

A church shivering
at night to music,
Saturday
before the feathered saint died
over bones,
his smiths pressed
a washing man
onto a door key.
I put the knots
a lady prayed
around my neck
to be clean
like our cousin
anointed
with the river.
A mountain lion
left her tracks
on the red tiles
we kneeled.
Hands bled
like wings
from the bite
of the field
to purify
the spring
with the wounds
of belief
like a lunatic
baptized by ashes
of falling leaves.

5.

Moon in the entrance
of a lake cavern
like torch fire lights
the skull
of a beautiful woman.
I rowed you
through the blue forest
of submerged trees
like the vertebrae
of flying owls.
The water rippled
like handwriting on paper
under your touch
of words obscured
by draperies of rain.

6.

Under a peeled ceiling
of magnolia flowers,
night clouds kept the streetlamps
red in a delirium
she shines for all
like the changing moon.
I go to the smoke
as three horses escape
the quiet white carvings
on her personal wall.

7.

On the mountain
I fired a rifle
at the sky bared
like a dog's tooth.
Stones pressed back
to the creek drip
like a cup of divination
to my tongue.
I spilled the water
from my head
to nurse a dead bird
leaving the earth
in a pile of feathers
we leapt.

8.

When I lifted
the white scarf
from your throat
your mouth opened
for a kiss
touching nothing
except itself
like rain on the bay.
The water of your arms
burnt fragrant tar
like sleep
I trailed blue.

9.

Washing basin
beneath a skylight
of rain.
Water cleaned my body
for a sickbed
of white sheets.
My unpacked suitcase
held mostly coins
and blood agate.
Your vervain oil
and cardamom seeds
I will always keep
to hide inside
your scent
like a blue nightgown.
The whale skull
of the ceiling
felt like sun
lifted stone
to let me breathe
and sleep
without pain
like lavender birds
escaping.

John Swain

10.

The moon pressed red
through a leopard
like a ritual sword drips
with a sea taste
into a chalice.
Then my face mirrored
the dark water
we dreamed
like a drowning
beneath summer trees.
Outstretch of your neck
raised the sky upward
like a drawn bow
to fall and become
the bed of our ground.

11.

Sunlight on a hawk's claw
turned like a coronet
as clouds shadow its body
marking the mountain
with our shapes together,
hawk head and limbs combined
on the mountain alone
between two raging bays.
The wilderness existing
overtook the house
of found metal at the summit
where we once slept.
Looking down
through the canyon
I startled at the wind sound,
my scrim face held the bright sky
stilled as the black flies bit
and drew blood
at my wrist I licked
like a horse.
Then the silent hawk
circled back like a ring
with another hawk
feet locked
above the sudden oak death
that whitened the entire landscape
with a hideous rot.
I found a fallen talon
cut red in my mouth to allow
the spirit's girl another birth
out of her wings soaring.

12.

Green books of bird paintings
line the white wall of shelves.
I hung a chaparral stick
that looked like a burnt wing
from the fan.
In the beauty of a clean room,
this glittering tree miniature
turned to smoke
dark as the voice I heard alone
inside your breast of earth.

13.

A bed of leaves
for the rain to sleep
the distant pain she looked away
with a shadow gown
around her feet.

14.

The deer scrape
for grass
on the lighthouse crag
above sea rolls
exposed
to the beautiful
astonishing wind
that you wore
like no clothes.
I felt the bells
sinking
like your shining
necklace pebbles
white and blue
to resume
our movement
like fish
beneath ships
calling the sun
from abyss
like a flower.

15.

Cupolas
above the sea
green chapel
of seal furs
and hanging bells.
I cast
a handful of ashes
to the water,
I scraped
the powder
from the smoke
on the face
of a black icon
crying
for all the dead
underneath
the day spiked
in the fire
we must turn
ourselves
to find.

16.

With glass to eye I scoured
burning islands
and rock arches
where the river
from the mountain
spilled to ocean
like a mystic
through four jagged pillars
shadowing sun
like blood
on a bear's claw
where the salmon returned.
I piled a bundle
of drifts like the shelter
of a burial ship
for the sea to take
like a dire god
of appetite.

John Swain

17.

Like wind into a bell
gulls ride the bright wave
and then air
over ecstatic shores.
Visitors miniature
the black rock formations
with cairns.
In sadness
I added a flat stone
and asked forgiveness
of myself.
The sea expanse
closed with fog
over the dry ridge
like a room of muted sun.
Then I slept
below a cross of hawks
as dawn perishes.

18.

Last October
I split my ring finger
with a knife
to give bones
and tendons
away like I lived
when I loved
a young girl wolf.
I sewed the close
with her brown hair
we traded
like vows
in the situation
we found
to be alone.

19.

Moon of fog
I watched
the heart-split hoof prints
disappear in snow woods.
I was swallowed in turn
by beasts of the mountain
I loved.
I filled a catamount track
with silver coins
I will always carry
like a relic
for strength
against the strength
I lost
to the effort ongoing
again like a person.
The sorcery of trees
transformed the path
with branches like wings
of the dead they conceal.
I scratched my skin
on the limbs
to receive thorn
opening a cavern
of buried voices
within the rock's shoulder.
Blood on twigs split
like a blossom of light
to be alive
inside God's maw.

20.

Apple sunlight
of the autumn
after years of dreaming
an empty tree
I had darkened
when a lion
like a woman
filled the tree
with its world.
I poured water
with lemons
and ginger
to recover
from spending
my rib gristle
to the air
of her mouth,
our beginning
like a tincture
from gardens
of black earth.

21.

River of wading
still channel
between the bank
and the island
of trees and rock.
Sun in the blood
every summer
to enter a shelter
composed of bones
hidden by roots
and branches.
The boat slowed
in the shallows
turning up mud.
We loosened
with the shove
of a green oar.
In the water
I wore a signet
of your interest
like protection
against the mouth
of its dark heart
swallowing arms
to hold itself close
as we travel.

John Swain

22.

Michigan in the woods
behind the sand dunes
leading to a red lighthouse,
a lady played a loon sound
as she walked through cedars.
Swimming in the lake
the raccoon turned around
to drown a hunting dog
by pressing its head under
the surface of tree shadows.
Thickets of berries sweeten
the tongue and perfume
her thorn torn leggings,
a thundercloud formed
around an owl's skull
like the heart of wild earth
reborn as it darkly wakens.
And again I fell in love
with the black downpour
the world had become.

John Swain

23.

Through the sycamore
I return to the water,
life my own to live again
with the ghost it holds
like a river.
Fireflies painted night
as the moccasin unhinged
its jaws like the sky
around your tree body
wreathed with grasses.
White feathered branches
mother the dead
in your skin
of the moon isolated
in repose for our cult.

24.

Refacing tomb effigies
of autumn trees
upon the quarried hillside,
a light in the sky
skeletonized the red hawk
above the river
pierced by its high wailing.
I stood
inside the shadow of bones
like a robe
on the littered shore
beside a white boat
and memorized the fires
from camps downstream.
The deer bent to drink
at the edge of a creek,
its soft neck
became a wooden arch
like a tree in dreams
where a hermit girl hanged
a black dress for each day
to dry
above the embers
of her forgotten body.

25.

The early dark
on white birch shines
to hide
its overcoming.
I kept the air
in a jar
to feed tea candles
in remedy.
Distant sleep
I reached
like the hood
over a crow's skull.
A blanket of flame
became enraged
by the perils
of your saint
I challenged
and allowed
to be my arms
like arrows
in your arms
of river trees.

26.

A lake of rain
still and moving
like an atrium
of liquid glass.
The secret eyes
of sleeping horses
in the trees
lit a brass lamp
for the mirror
when I poured
more clear water
for no memories
of the ocean.

27.

I watched the harbor
change colors
in the rain and fog.
The emerald curve
of the waves
churning sand
looked like blood
crashing on the rock.
The sea pressed me
to the wall
of a volcanic heart
dead for eons
now guarding
falcons at its height.
The mist sprayed
like disembodied heads
speaking for the witch
of this island.

28.

The gathered trees filled with wind
moving like deer from the arrows.
Skulls lined the ancient body
of a warrior hawk with black wings
folded over the mountain.
Daybreak came with the moon
still looming over my shoulder
and I embraced the dynamic being
that a photograph only diminishes.
The fullness of loving is momentary
like a woman with child transforms
the unknown of the dark feeding dark
like a shadow
over the fire road to the open coast.

John Swain

29.

Torches hang
from the moon tree
like white fruit
to your white dress
and knife
I embroidered
with fumes
of burnt silver.
I piled
the branches again
for your glory
in the body
above us
so distant
and intimate
as a miracle
like the scapular
of a falcon
attached
to the fire air
at your back
opening
another sky
of delight
in the smoke
of kindling
as it takes you
to raise
from the gallery
of feral actors
in sackcloth
after the farce
of our trial.

30.

Wind from the sea field
we entered like an armor
then all the world was blue
as our receding
from faces
like a tide of recovery
from each metamorphosis
of the ocean.
Pillbugs fed
upon the gray head
of a buried gull
like a moon floating under
the sand and surf as water
becomes a darkness
guarded by monsters.
A written spell
from your tongue
in the mask of a black dog
made us as water
like a passage
to the underworld
in endless forgetting
of each wave initiated
by rituals of air
we exchanged to taste
like a salt in pure elixir.

31.

The rain will rain
over the gray birds
of a privacy
we leave alone.
The sky darkened
a confining wall
like the border
of mourning paper
we wrote
to say nothing
and let the action
of the craft
elaborate our praise
and resignation
as the nail
sealed the wood
against your breasts
like a fine dress
buried in the air
of our houses.

Smith

When John asked me to write a poem a day I said no because my normal 10-20 poems per month had dropped to one poem in 7 weeks.

But later riding my bicycle through crackling dried fall leaves I found a haiku for day 1. 161 days later I have a new poem written and posted each day. Plan to stop March 31 with 6 months and 182 poems. Going to try to stop the 31st because it's become an obsession, albeit one that has rewarded me with a plethora of surprises. I've found each succeeding month's poems to be superior to the previous, so these 31 are the bottom of this barrel.

— *Smith, 3.10.2014*

Wood Smoke in Chill Air

The cusp of the crisp
leaves dry fallen crinkle
beneath bicycle wheel

— 10.1.2013

Hey Heisenberg

Thanks for the poem and the stone
and the Lady and the cat
and just in general for the way it's at.

My downs are shallow my ups way deep
though my following's fallow
my adventures are neat.

I'm not gloating just grateful
for growing up in the 50's poor but loved
well fed from 40-acre farm life led.

Friends galore my galoshes for soul
what's more they tend me toward the whole
keep angry arrogance from being more so.

I whine along my way but have to say
in retrospect it's been fun, rich in roast
high in spent, a sweet sweat scent adventure.

— 10.2.2013

Steven Smith

Political Potty

You don't miss your dirt till the ground runs wet
Don't scuff your shoes until the hounds are let
Don't pay for those until these are gone
Don't use condoms in hope of more spawn

They say east is west and orange new black
Yet forget the fact that tack lacks slack
But talk enough in their double tongue
Reveals true depth by showing none

Their shallow end's too deep for them
These minimal unmemorable men
Whose yes or no slides so for pay
Who pray what those above say they play

Stop is go and go got gone
It's been a lie all along
They change the words after each scene
And claim it didn't mean a thing

But next time for sure they'll get it right
And swear for rare they'll play fair
Yet it's Three-Card Monte every night
Hide this under that right here over there

Been fooled for once, been fooled for twice
Be thinking this stinking fooling ain't nice

— 10.3.2013

Hear as song:
reverbnation.com/mutantsmith/song/18891505-political-potty

Steven Smith

23 magnetic refrigerator words x 2

I.
For egress
wild subterfuge of dust
and juggernaut passion
never languish
with latex electric alacrity

Psychedelic tantamount
& echelon
you have onyx
shard

II.
Psychedelic alacrity
subterfuge of shard onyx egress
you have dust wild juggernaut & tantamount passion
with electric echelon and languish latex
for never

— *10.4.2013*

Steven Smith

Tellavision

Crowded waiting room
too many life forms
too much about not enough

For rights sake
put some lotion on your emotion
mix mambo in the mar
drink up then downsize the potion
set for sun and slip the sale
leave lunch pill pail
life's a mix of mush and moxy
higher your ethic brighter your star
fame is three times five-minute epoxy
once we flee the shadows of were

— 10.5.2013

Guvmnt Job

Well now guess I ain't gonna be
getting me one of them there govmnt jobs
since my dissatisfaction with our foreign policy
classifies me as a potential traitor
and they may be right I just might
be a danger to government lies
since I think things like
maybe we shouldn't be invading other folk's countries
and maybe it ain't nice going round
killing anybody we feel like with our drones
but hey, that's just me and my moral upbringing
which was taught to me by Americans . . .
uh, wait a minute,
something wrong here
cuz how can the folk who told me it ain't nice to kill
be going around doing all this killin' and torturin' and invadin'
and lyin' and cheatin' and treason?????????????

— 10.6.2013

Steven Smith

Mea Culpa

These are interesting times
what with print lessening as digital explodes,
petroleum economy dying while clean energy grows,
climate change changing crop, insect, population pattern,
citizens rising against politician corporation,
white males in decline as diversity blooms
increasing life-style and gender companion awareness,
meat poisoning exploding even as healthy eating increases,
life spans and decent jobs and incomes declining,
baby deaths approaching third world levels,
prisons stuffed for profit,
economic inequality,
mass extinctions,
sexism, racism . . .
so much to do,
so many opportunities,
but what an awkward world
for the foot draggers, the knuckle scrappers, the deniers.

I understand pain
wish to add fewer ripples to wave
as I backslide my way to better.

— 10.7.2013

Was the Sound of One Zen Clown

Life is what you do with what you got
Get hit too hard, walk it off
Eat too much, pack on the lard
Just work the load and walk it off
Do the daily shilly-shally
Bet the nag, chew wacky tobacky
Prioritize lies, check the whys
Repeat replies
It's never enough so walk it off
Talk soft, walk it off
Chalk cross, walk it off
Held aloft, walk it off
Sugar gumball close to crock
Willie nilly silly willy
Best just walk it off
This is Zen the Clown here talkin'
You're shadow loose if you don't start walkin'

— 10.8.2013

Steven Smith

Happy Trails 2 U

I wouldn't be silly today
if I hadn't dropped so much psilocybin along the way.

Now keep my silly sighs in silly sigh bins
sometime try em on for sizes.

My fame is secret cuz nobody knows
(cuz everyone nos).

Looking through the Zens, trying not to focus.

Ahhhhhh . . . clean body, clean bed, clean sheets new fed.

May thou flow go well, swell be thee and thine.

— *10.9.2013*

Indian Summer

Girls wear curls
And squirrels whirl
Oh what a ride we are

— 10.10.2013

Out at the In-laws 4

Three hours northeast to Pennsylvania fading light
on squiggle line no-name lanes
with no street signs most times
and those that do don't agree with GPS
their there not matching our near
which is how horror movies start
but we get there
stare into night fire
thoughts rise like sparks in squid ink sky
no street light no house store traffic
no water electricity toilet
no cell phone home
no people or city sky near by
just trees we can't see
in black bear crossing
moon peek through leaf
black bean burger cowboy coffee
charred iron griddle pole-swung over flame
toast bagels in fire
potatoes, bacon, eggs
foil-wrapped ear corn on coals
steroidal marshmallow on stick
chill woodsmoke from past
woodpecker tapping
ax split wood wedgie
s'mores, hobo pies, devil's dung,
sleep deep dark
new rise early
stroke smolderfire
secret toke
coffee
sneak up on black bear
"Tsk-tsk-tsk" its retreating back
till it stops, looks over shoulder
I say soft slow low Just want a better foto
to its shuffle off and gone
but at least it looked me in the eye and listened.

— 10.11.2013

Steven Smith

Trees We Helped Plant Today

Black Cherry
Red Oak
Hop Hornbeam
Tulip Poplar
Black Walnut
Sycamore
Hackberry
American Hornbeam
Ohio Buckeye
Black Gum
Swamp White Oak
Pin Oak
Silky Dogwood

350 trees planted
we dug 15 holes in earthy heal
blue sun sky above
fall leaf forest before us

— 10.12.2013

Steven Smith

Tinkledown Economics

Do what you want
Take what you want
It's all all right if you don't get caught

The rich boys dance
without their pants
their ding dongs dangle
as they prance

I pray to Great Gosh
O my Gosh
Run - the future is coming !

— 10.13.2013

Deconstructing Cyborg Smith

1950s: once a year I'd rip flesh open
and parents would dash me to town for stitches.

1969: first operation, deviated septum.

1976: second operation, nut-cut sterilized.

1977: collar bone, ribs break, crack pelvis.

1985: fall down hill, break both wrists both elbows.

1989: squishy movable blob cut from finger.

1991: alcohol crash burn bled to death, woke in ICU.

2005: cancer cut from voice box

2006: 8 weeks radiation
2006: throat biopsy and removal of nose polyps
which filled my head eye socket to brain pan

2008: hernia operation left side.

2011: right hip replacement.

2012: hernia operation right side.

2013: all but 8 lower teeth removed.
2013: all upper teeth removed.
2013: bone spur cut from upper jaw (today).
2013: in three weeks, voice box bump cut out,
biopsied, await outcome. →

Steven Smith

Synthetic mesh in left groin,
more mesh in right,
titanium ball and screw and ceramic socket in hip,
metal plastic eye glasses,
plastic upper teeth and metal plastic partial.

Welcome to Cyborg Smithworld.
I now set metal detectors off in courthouses, airports.

Lady's searching for my receipt and warrantee,
just to see
but says she plans on keeping me.

I'm one-of-a-kind prototype anyway,
factory decided not to proceed with production.
For obvious reasons.

So if you want to meet the real me
best hurry
before there's less be to see.

— *10.14.2013*

Steven Smith

Wife is white blossom
I but branch of sun in wind
Together we be tree

— 10.15.2013

Insect Sex

Insects stop sex when storms approach
cuz buzz 'n wiggle ain't no giggle
when raindrops falling are as big as a fridge
so for simple survival
no fug bucking if storm coming

Now as for human sects
they fug all the time.

— 10.16.2013

Steven Smith

Wordworn

At the Bookstore on 25th St
after reading one of my better poems,
a woman asked,
"Is that a real poem, or did you write that?"

Entering Lake Erie Bookstore
I inquired, "Where would I find Bukowski?"
"Probably drunk in an alley somewhere in L.A."
the proprietor replied.

Walking home, the foghorn calling.
Dark and damp, early rainy morning.

— 10.17.2013

Sunrise Service

The sun
rises through dry
tree leaves as the birds check
our feeder for seeds, leaving song
in thanks

— *10.18.2013*

Wordslinger

I once
rode the cinquain
slow train from town to town
to sling as few words possible
for gain.

Being
fastest quip in
town, in two-tongue silver
I mowed them down with metaphor
galore.

My sly
sounds and clever
cuts and quick slice to the
Id grid made no one butter, got
no grits.

Cut ups,
put downs, just sounds
fed from fear or folly,
foul feature far from formless foe,
worthless.

Never
a where to go,
a want to be, a way
to see fair a free and easy
future.

So words
of scold in old
I let go, their sorrow

Steven Smith

sent and said in some hot blood red
of err.

Someone's
always faster,
meaner, so go slow, nice,
it throws them off, perverts their pace,
wins race.

Better
yet, don't compete
to feed the seed of need
in heat of hate that self relates
in each.

— *10.19.2013*

When WHAM

Rainy day gray away
from light and warmth and sun
drive 90 minutes south
to Main Street Mansfield
for Lady's poetry feature
read and listen 100 minutes
drive 110 minutes north
to Mac's Backs Coventry
for yearly Poetry w/out Walls tribal gathering
when **WHAM**
turn turn signal on move left
when **WHAM**
slow and stop and wait for traffic
when **WHAM**
sit there 60 seconds
when **WHAM**
Jeep woman behind us hits brake
tires lock in hydroplane on rained plain
WHAMS our car
WTF?
not even moving
2 minutes from parking
3 minutes from picking up dinner
(and me finally pissing 3rd cup coffee)
5 minutes from the poetry people
our brand-new used hybrid
the newest near-new I've known
and wife's apple eye
cries a tear with violent rear smear
bumper totaled hatch bent
but for bad to be had
it went swell well
Jeep woman's words
"Are you hurt? Are you all right? I'm so sorry"
shows she's nice, →

Steven Smith

honest,
no one's injured,
she's insured,
confesses,
young cop's decent,
car's drivable if we don't drive fast
Jeep's unscathed
so good went bad
but bad fair good as badlands go
and though not sure of what or why or whether
I'm just glad it's not my fault
because in the once upon it would of.

— 10.20.2013

Said the Strider to the Why

Step into my spider said the parlor to the fly
It's warm with moistened sloping to its gentle lie
She'll fit you with a jacket of her finest weave
Of course she'll keep insisting you can never leave

The cost is oh so simple
Your life and nothing less
The heft of spin is ample
To keep you in this mess

The sin of mother's father
And father's other friend
Leads the gland to funnel
Fear to smother end

No use in checking exit
Your fly friends are all gone
All that matters you exist
And fit my baking pan

So come up free and easy to my loft in sky
Sit and sip your sorrow as I set my sly
At least you'll find some purpose in my flying pan
Your essence keeps me going, your spirit fulls my fan

— *10.21.2013*

Hear as song:
reverbnation.com/mutantsmith/song/18982059-said-the-spider-mix-b

Entropy

The leaves
beneath my feet
crack dry sun and shadow
as I walk unready from warmth
to cold

— 10.22.2013

Steven Smith

E.T. Call Home

Just asked cat if she were a litter critter?
A fur cur?
A purr fur?
Or fur purr?
She came over
let me pet her,
but didn't actually answer.

— *10.23.2013*

Letter to Maj Ragain

Hmmmm, am I persevering . . . . ?
persevere is what I do.
I smile in joy and joy continue
or reign anger and smile continue.
Try to find path of compassion and patience
but sometimes think
they handed me the wrong map.
Yet overall, more joy than not,
more grateful than not.
Glad I'm me.
Glad you're you.
Still trying to find the hungry ghost's tackle box.
Love you lots.

— 10.24.2013

Natural Geographic

Honey in the bee box
Raisins in the bread
Found my baby cooking
Took her back to bed
Asked her in the morning
How she liked my beats
Said I was a poet
But need to test more sheets
Rode her to the mountain
Nestled in the cloud
Down to bushy plain
Where the field is plowed
Played her wet in water
Held her high in air
Laughed like loonies liking
Then took her to the fair
Climbed among the Tetons
Rubbed around the mill
Reaching each our reasons
Scrubbed a rub the grill
Not much more to mutter
Matters not at all
That we bit the apple
That led us to this fall

— 10.25.2013

Hear as songs:
reverbnation.com/mutantsmith/song/19039565-natural-geo
reverbnation.com/mutantsmith/song/19039553-natural-geographic

Steven Smith

Fusion

Dead man's music plays
the night, electric Miles
in a silent way

Old music in strange
clothes soft and sweet sweep beat
with new ears

— *10.26.2013*

Tin Wouldman

Art heart thou art, Tin Woodman
thy empty space outfilling place you rest
in exo-tin softer than calloused skin
firm fondness felt for care to spare
beware the eye of other
their chitinous text
firm beating flesh bereft of heft
in immoral press of next for blood and turnip
spurn it and them Tin Wouldman
friend indeed
you are much heeded
though heartless thou art heart
and bleed for need when needed

— 10.27.2013

By Sin of Reason Worship

Forgive me O Great Furthur
for I sin in seeking logic
in your willful whirl.

I prod cause for effect,
weigh the yea and nay of yes and no,
move for right unwrung from wrong
so sin in reason worship.

No selling sacrificial fire
with need, want, wish, won't,
in burn of flower radish.

Instead weigh
the good and bad of ugly.

So tell you what
I let it go
you warp and woof your winning season
but I'm off this bended knee
to grieve my own weave.

We'll pretend your random matters
but I plant my seed in fairer furrow.

— 10.28.2013

Steven Smith

Holy Martin Luther, Batman ! ! !

(quotes by Martin Luther, 1483-1546, father of the Protestant religion)

You dear asses. You poisonous loudmouth. You are jugglers of imaginary sins. I would not smell the foul odor of your name. You are a bungling magpie, croaking loudly. All you say is sealed with the devil's own dirt. Snot-nose! My soul, like Ezekiel's, is nauseated at eating your bread covered with human dung. Do you know what this means? You are a little pious prancer. You have a perverted spirit that thinks only of murdering the conscience. You should rightly be called lawyers for asses. If you are furious, you can do something in your pants and hang it around your necks - that would be a musk apple and pacem for such gentle saints. You condemned the holy gospel and replaced it with the teaching of the dragon from hell. You reek of nothing but Lucian, and you breathe out on me the vast drunken folly of Epicurus. You vulgar boor, blockhead, and lout, you ass to cap all asses, screaming your heehaws. You are spiritual scarecrows and monk calves. I am tired of the pestilent voice of your sirens. Your Hellishness. You are one of those bloody and deceitful people who affect modesty in words and appearance, but who meanwhile breathe out threats and blood. Your home, once the holiest of all, has become the most licentious den of thieves, the most shameless of all brothels, the kingdom of sin, death, and hell. It is so bad that even Antichrist himself, if he should come, could think of nothing to add to its wickedness. You have set out to rub your scabby, scurvy head against honor. We should not only refuse to obey you, but consider you insane or criminals. I think that all the devils have at once entered into you. Take care, you evil and wrathful spirits. God may ordain that in swallowing you may choke to death. What else can one say here, except that these ideas originate in your own wanton concoctions, or in a drunken dream? A seven-year-old child, indeed, a silly fool, can figure it out on his fingers - although you, stupid ass, cannot understand anything. I am tired of the pestilent voice of your sirens. You are ignorant, stupid, godless blasphemers. You pant after the garlic and melons of Egypt and have already long suffered from perverted tastes. Phooey on you, you servant of idols! I must stop: I can no longer rummage in your blasphemous, hellish devil's filth and stench.

— 10.29.2013

Steven Smith

Reading Room

Reading Auden in the living room,
Stevens in the john.
Good to sit, good to go.

— *10.30.2013*

Steven Smith

The Not O.K. Corral

If my name were Who
and I knocked at your door
and you called "Who's there?"
and I replied "Right"
what would you do?

I mean the O.K. Corral might have been okay
for Wyatt Earp and Doc Holliday say
but not so okay if you look
Claiborne, Clanton, McLaury's way
(30 shots, 30 seconds, 6 feet apart, 3 guys gone)

I believe Guantanamo is male,
whereas Guantanamera is female . . .
though I'm too poor for a parasite,
can only afford a single site.

Our new lies are 17% more factual than our old lies.

The Princess had no pea
so I offered her my rumpled foreskin.

Whoa mama,
better get that skitter tied down
before it departs.

Coco Chanel never wore flannel.
Though women wear falsies, men wear false he's.

Is the plural of men menses?

Lady was bargaining with me
so I called her a Berber woman
as did the Berber vendor in Morocco
when she bargained him below her original offer.

Steven Smith

She told me, "No, I'm not cold at all,
but if you keep pummeling me with puns,
I'm going to need a punbrella."

Life is hard, and then you climax.

Wanted for unrest - the Coffee Kid.
I'm serving time in the plenum-tentiary.
My odds are getting odder,
especially from the otters,
not to mention others.

I dye lemma, for I am my own lexeme.
All godz chillun gots problems.

Ah yes, the lesser of evils . . .
could be a business opportunity here
for if I had two evils
and rented them by the hour,
I'd be the leaser of two evils.

Hello weirdness my old friend
I'd welcome you back again,
but you never left.

The United Mutations of Smith now in session,
the Irreverend me presiding.

Take your time.
No hurry.
Heal.
Be well.
Sorry bout the broken bits.

— 10.31.2013

Steven Smith

Lady

October 2013 was one of the hardest months I've ever had in my life. It was hard for a lot of people. Our government was not operating well. We were in danger of default.

The craziness started a couple days before October 1st. And on the first, John Burroughs asked me to participate in this massive poetry project.

I paced the first week thinking about nature, about bees, about the weather, about the wolves, about our civilization's honeycomb hive. Nature's tendrils twirled around my keyboard and heart, bowstring taut fraught.

As October 17th drew near, I thought about what it would mean to feel relief, to not have to be burdened by the government's craziness anymore. I prayed and prayed. I bled relief from my wellspring of hope. When the 17th came, I bled gratitude.

As the fraughtness collapsed our auto was smacked. We were coming from a poetry reading and going into a parking lot for another when we felt the $6000 crunch behind us.

I lost a major web account, monthly money.

I had three days of not sleeping well.

I remembered something that was very important I had pushed away so as to not deal with it. My husband had something in his throat. It's OK, now, but it was a hard thing.

My nails still show October. They were healthy going in, longer than they'd ever been, and coming out, flaking and discolored.

But I got some decent poems.

— Lady

TRUST

Like a trapeze artist flying from one swing to another

A spider floating and flying on its web

A climber finding purchase on a rock

So much bounty found

Someone just trusting herself
to walk into the next day with ease

So many days are with ease
and I wrinkle my walnut over nothing
remember, little primate brain:

Trust

Do good

Be good

I'm lucky

Many are

Friends there for us

Family there, too

Discount none

Be taken care of
reasonably well

Take care of what I can →

Me help Great Protector
Great Protector helps me when It can

Great Big nurturing mama nipples of Reality
papa arms, grandpa leading little girl in dance,
little feet atop big foot, grandma who says
I love you in a million ways

The surprising blessings from siblings,
dividends of cousins discovered,
yearning for daughters, sons, nieces, nephews

The learning of this yearning!

I trust

I rail and tantrum
I have my anxieties
yet sometimes I remember

Breathe...

And I trust

In God I find myself
surprised!
to trust

— *October 1, 2013*

LOVELY WEATHER WE'RE HAVING

It's October 2013 now
and rather humid

The sky is dark
more of the time,
but it's warm
& crickets
still sing their
sonic blanket

I'm glad for the bees
for they collect more goldenrod
in this extended summer,
the summer
that didn't get very hot
but lasted a long time,
faded in and out

A summer that is now
into autumn

I'll gladly trade
warmer here
for enough cold
in the Arctic

I paint my nails
with snow-colored polish

Layer of ice,
layer of snow,
help it along

Arctic snow
in my mind   →

for there

Bees on my mind

for here
& everywhere
they bee

Bees with honey harvest
bounty for biding

I wonder what it's like,
a bee in a hive
in an Ohio winter

They suck honey,
keep queen & babies warm
vibrate wings
to heat home hive—
93 degrees!

Not an icebox, that

What do the songs of their
wings sound like, what shruti songs,
what keys, chords,
tones, melodies?

What dreams?

— October 2, 2013

PROCESS

There's material material
and stuff that seems immaterial
yet casts its rebar into
material material

The immaterial encourages

Some of that template-making stuff
is not so pleasant. Should be rubbish
rather than cast. Be it from ego turned
to vinegar, it's refuse

Self-esteem fine, but loft turned to
creepy vintage stinky craven stuff—
let's make it dregs, rather than mold
of errant mode

It's rubble from process
the shape of where I put myself
intermediately in slice of Long Now

It's audience the ego wants
Some type of netting for its vine
so it can grow up and up and up

Audience &/or peace? How to be tame
through all this gym?

Magician runs self through
such long hoops,
days and years of them

Poet communicator

Artist for various balms →

Sage at rest when needed

Sighing, the different ways
parts of my day feel

The alchemy that makes them
be it natural or learn-ed

— October 3, 2013

FLOW FLUX GRIND

Grinds pay time
with hard work

Gravity-soaked hard work

Or hard work
in the anti-gravity machine
pinioned between
sculptures &
their honest tools
to meet the moment

Whatever Reality tides in from
non-local locality
is quickly spackled
into Rat Nest brain

Grind.

Grind punctuated by free flow moments
when Squirrely-Grind looks up
from her nest

Sees slices of Heaven
in the living room of her space ship

Assured it's there any time
she needs it

— October 4, 2013

MAN REAL

Where are you on your computer besides under it,
my husband points his finger at me, asks.

Where are you in your head besides in your head?
Are you on your feet? Does your head rest on your
neck, is your neck comfortable (I hope so)?

Does your back feel good? Is the lumbar region
well-supported?

It feels so good to breathe, yes?

It feels so good.

Are you taking care of yourself? Are you choosing
to hone your tone
with honey crisp apples?

The clatter of domesticity in the kitchen
is so nice, yeah? And then subsequent footsteps
with platter of food, industriousness
sinking into the lazyboy,
accretion of realizations into
long-lasting balm,
man real.

— October 5, 2013

SONG BIRDS

Blessings of birds
miscellaneous chatter

Whatever makes them choose
one tree over another

Ohio sparrows

Glad they're not sparse

Passerines

"Bird Girl" by
Antony and the Johnsons
assures me I'll
go to Heaven

All Bird Girls
go to Heaven

And if one's anxious
to experience it,
just walk under
trees

Hear ornaments
of fluttering sounds
twisting and hopping

Cheerful by virtue
of vocabulary

Aiming for what
nestled purchase
claims

— *October 6, 2013*

SUN DANCE

Maybe the sun knows exactly
how it'll look
to all involved
at all moments
with various plays
light through leaves
mackerel sky sunset

Sun on the moon, making it bright
first star first star I see in daylight
wish I well, wish I delight

This star engine
casts large energy releases,
solar flares

Strung honey
in the maw
of field

It boils and roils gently
for such glorious hot enormity

Source injecting lightfood
for complexity

Bees in the lattice
of the magic

Fruit and foot
bloom
in the current medium

— October 7, 2013

AGENTS FOR A HAPPY LIFE

I'd like to see a wild bees' nest
I think of them as part of the trees—well, and part
of everything—the sun and other stars

Agents of wooded network
tendrils of fur, feather and claw
so many soft and hard fruits

Agents of themselves
agents of fecundity, art

They are my parents, bees—
and my children

On my table
I would like some foods
for all time through all time any time:
honey, bread, fruit, nuts, legumes,
a vat of fat I can spread with a knife

My kitchen is a crumb factory
evidence of a mostly happy life
fresh linens, pots and pans

In Heaven we'll have lots of time

We'll go on expeditions for those
wild bees' nests

Wild bees without stress
who'll just let us
reach into their combs
fill our jars
with butter knives
for gingham picnics   →

We can do some of this now,
you know

— *October 8, 2013*

HONEY IN THE BEE BOX

Honey in the bee box
honey in the bee box
honey...

Honey in the bee box
honey in the bee box
honey...

Sun Ra sings
"Honey in the Bee Box"
on the album
"Interplanetary Melodies"
and I wonder
what are bees like
on other planets?

There must be bees
on other planets,
beads who string fruit
from flower
to mouth

I've seen
people's visions
of alien flowers and fruit

If vision be Reality
on some intuitive level

Taiko drum vision
thunking engines of the stars
with wild gladness

Seeds and semen into
Mother Nature's yen

— October 9, 2013

POMERANIANS

Relax,
I tell myself

Pretend you are a limp noodle
or something just sated & sitting
or even gently walking
running

Take the knot that's occupied your mind
and push it away when it gets tight

That puzzle that you like to work on—
don't get strung up in it

Take the hairy thing and behold it
in your mind's hands and lap

Settle for the math of wholeness,
parse fractions out of the fur,
brush the burrs off the Pomeranian

It's OK to throw out the burrs
I know you like to think about
everything from start to finish
to start

The life cycle of matter and ideas

But for groundedness's sake, just
let it loose
sometimes

It's alright! Say uncle!

Even let the Pomeranians →

Lady

run loose with all the burrs
they can find

Other people are dealing
with the issues

Just relax!

Take your time
sip and sup
sleep, unwind
let stress go
relax the center
of the universe

— *October 10, 2013*

IN THIS BIG DREAM REALITY

In this big dream reality

In the little dreams that are
like little wakenings

I find my true abilities, long-lost,
finally remembered

I fly

Some of them start off
with my flying
and they're easy
but then I look
and I wonder,
wow, what is this
I am doing?
A human? flying?

And then I lose
the ability to
steer,
I careen
towards the land,
I can't get it up
more than a couple inches

And some
of the dreams start off with
my flying rather clumsily
and then having to be
contained
by ceilings

The humans around me don't fly

They seem unsurprised

Jaded in the face of the miraculous

Miracles they've never seen
except in movies

I hover over their heads,
daring them to notice

I'm usually beautiful
in these dreams

But still, they don't notice

Maybe it's because I'm
spirit
hovering with bird

Maybe I'm just flying
with the bird
and humans see
the bird
and it's not remarkable
to them

And to think!

Birds!

They come from dinosaurs!

How different
can you get!

How amazing
the transformation!

Such miracles!

And so unremarked →

by so many

Veins
of untapped
realization

I'm glad people have

epiphanies

to discover

— October 11, 2013

BIRDS

I don't know much about birds
weird, for being a nature lover

My reality of names and sounds
is like a kids' coloring book
as far as the lexicon provided,
a fast food menu of facts

I'm working on it, tho

I'd like to drum up some more knowledge
in that writhing wrinkled walnut brain of mine
all the birds in the area, all the birds
that's what I want to know
and then moving on to more areas
might take me a hundred years

Their sounds...

I didn't even know how a blue jay sounds
or anything other than perhaps
the cooing of pigeons
as far as being able to pin the tail
on the donkeybird goes

It was like this vast miraculous
soup of sound to me—still is—

But now I know blue jays, robins
song sparrows...

Blue jays go raw, raw, raw, raw, raw
like what you think a crow might do

And robins go →

cheerup, cheerup, cheerup,
pretty bird, pretty bird, cheerup, cheerup, cheerup

And song sparrows
chip chip chip chip chip chee chee chee
chip chip chip chip chip chee chee chee
chip chip chip chip chip chee chee chee
chee chee chee chee

And they all have their
introspective muttering
ruminations, too

— *October 12, 2013*

THE THINKING CLOUD

She's very much like us,
I told my husband, who was
holding our companion cat

She has feelings too,
and she's sitting there thinking
while in your arms

I don't know if she has any words
in her head, I said

But she thinks—be it in
words, image, feelings

I wonder what she thinks about,
he said

I think she thinks about what
we think about, I said, and we're
actually in a thinking cloud

The thinking cloud is all around
us, I said, and we just operate
in it

Do we have any different thoughts?
he asked

We might have individualized takes
on the topics that the
thinking cloud is thinking
but much of it is the thinking cloud

There might be some unique stuff though
depends on what we tune in to   →

Lady

Aliens stole my brain, he said

Ah, no worries, I said
It's all in the cloud

— *October 13, 2013*

BRIGHT MOON

Bright moon
over cities
something cosmopolitan
seemingly striated with lanes

Bright moon

Irregardless of heat or coolness here

Bright moon

Free light show

Bright moon
in the fields

Bright moon
through growing lace
the reaching of forests,
candle through the wood
that does not burn

Bright moon
over neighbor's roof

Early morning
big box present sky
reminds me
put the cat on the sill
sit in the chair

Experience
happy amenities
of now

— October 14, 2013

HAPPINESS TREATY

Come home to now—

Rebuild family and
protect Mother Earth!

This is how to be home,
says Thich Nhat Hanh

I notice the features
of our landscape
and the tools
of this "home" vocabulary

Working and reworking,

(clumsily at first—
tight ordinances remembered)
but

Being home...
as a meticulous janitor
as a craftsperson
cleaning up my mistakes
polishing what good's
been wrought

I'm finding my peace,
community building
like an excavation

An excavation uncovering
how special
friends are

I would like to turn gently →

from one to another

Friend where features

meet the sky
and friend
the points to the border
in every direction

Make my ears like
listening pillows
not smothering,
but where expressions
can come to rest

Pillows for capacitance
days of...

Like Thich Nhat Hanh says
turn back to one gently
a well-considered, sensitive
yet unsuffered response
from the factory of smoothness

I've learned gentleness

I'm working on
remembering it

For my sangha of health,
community of cheer

— *October 15, 2013*

RELIEF

I am mostly happy

Relief

When I look up
or inwards
or down or
outwards

or wherever…

to realize this

Realizing this repeatedly
pleasant mini-epiphanies

I am excited by the moment

I feel myself rushing in
more, more, more

Who can I tell about this,
like the excitement of
restless legs
I search and search
but what I seek
is most oft right here

I think this is why
it's a bit difficult
sometimes
to get my raft
to settle by the banks
under the overhang
of gentle branches

→

Relief

Even when I run, practiced pace
letting my store of consciousness
move my legs, smooth flow
rely on experienced breath

Relief

When I walk
earn feel-good chemicals
flooding my ruddiness

I am arriving,
Thich Nhat Hanh says

I am arriving,
I am here

Relief

When I work
spending time doing
what I plan
to do

Relief

When I relax
slack on the couch
no agenda
for the moment

Relief →

In the rain
cozy in my nest
glad for so many roofs
all over
doing their jobs

Relief

In the sun
BIG part of God
sending its energy...
massage...
into my warmed...
skin

(Major feel-good chemical release)

Relief

I trust

I do my parts
as best
I can discern

I anticipate
with gentle faith
and find I've
good reason
to do so

— October 16, 2013

MAKING GOOD

Here's the church
here's the steeple
open the doors &
here are the people...

Fingers
reach and come through
the interlace of play splay

Fingers do work
make promises

Fingers hold them, too

Fingers can point:
there's the interface
of human, goodness,
indices to ideals
signpost

And hands—
hands raised in class
folded together in prayers
hands illustrating concepts,
gesturing

Handshakes
good as words

Words
good as actions

Making good
tilling the field →

for crops of
good handshakes,
actualized

Physical vocabulary

Action absolute

— *October 17, 2013*

GRATITUDE

Gratitude

A type of water
a bath

We can bathe

We can wash our minds
help cleaned stuff
emerge

Not brainwash in the sense of
being hoodwinked

But wash
our minds
in the sense of
relief
honest relief

And so accessible,
gratitude

There's just so much to be grateful for
billions of things—infinite, actually—
to be grateful for

All the steps that are necessary
to get me to where I'm at
sitting on the sofa
typing this poem
thinking how
our cat companion
Mandy
is entree to many of my   →

realizations
of how I can be
so happy at any point
or at least
comforted
if I choose

Gratitude
when I realize there're
at least
some
parts of me
definitely good

Like how I
am rooting for y'all
happy to hear
yr success stories

Gratitude

It's like a big hairy root
growing right into the plenum,
the plenum nutrition

The water
in the plenum
plenum,
too

— October 18, 2013

SKY SHOWS

There was no
Cleveland Air Show
per se
this year

But we have
better air shows
anyways

Wings celebrate
The Everyday

Birds herald it
swoop down to illustrate
God's eyelash here
flying some smiley
emoticon

Flying creatures
the first to be buoyed
in grace of relief
passing from furied storm
to curtains opening
to portal of light

Sun sticking
its head in
to make a cameo
saw ya, see ya

Long moments on the road
we're given these
sky shows
from Sky God   →

Forcing us to enjoy
nature's nutrition
for the eyes
on our hurried
commutes

How many
see how
interesting
it all is
the detailed resolution
of the Dream
that's around us?

— *October 19, 2013*

CHOOSING TRACKS

I'm doing a mix tape
for you

I'm making a mix tape
that never gets boring
tap tap taps you into
calmness, then bliss
sans titillation

Maybe an ecstatic state
without frenzy, with only
a taste of the memory of angst
for comparison

But not
the actual
experience
of angst

Where anguish is
transformed into zest
such that every taste
tongue, touch, sound
is gently enough

That the passage
through days is gently
wonderfully enough

Chock with gusto
painless poignancy

You'll know for sure
you're cool like Blondie
hot like Bowie   →

as loosely flowing
yet contained
as Kate Bush

You'll know
you're forgiven
if that's what it takes
redeemed into goodness
if redemption necessary

You'll be as smiley
as the Dalai Lama as wise a
Thich Nhat Hanh

We'll all know it
but that won't matter

This is how I'll trick out the tape
and it won't be a trick

It's a prescription
for your wellbeing

And when you
can't listen
it'll have saturated
you
anyways

— October 20, 2013

HOW SALAD STARTS TO ARRIVE

Someone prepares soil
compost, aeration,
vitamins for baby plants

Someone plants the seeds
lettuce, pepper, tomato, radish, onion—
whatever people want

Time passes

You can see the time-lapse film
sun goes down, moon comes up
sprouts come up and follow the light rotations

Little leaves quiver, shake themselves open,
unfurl and pulse in larger and longer
bunchings of themselves

Baby plants grow
rain waters, sun coaxes
warm humidity encouraging
wonderfully monstrous growth spurts
vegetable nutrition from fecund soil

Hands come to collect lettuce leaves
turned over in unique fingerprints, palms

Soil shook loose
the resistance of clinging
rootedness

Plucked

Bundles taken to middlepeople
or sold directly in farmer's markets, farm shares   →

so pretty on the tables

We come with our french basket
and our bikes, a fair way
to spend an evening

For cultivation
of delightful lives
this is one way
salad
starts to arrive

— October 21, 2013

REMEMBERING WHAT I'VE LEARNED

My main issue
is with my mind and body
this is what makes me feel
one way and another

My mind palpable
buzzing and tight or
relaxed and fluid
and the associated
feelings in the body
that contribute to that
or are caused by it
feedback and
feedforward
multiple ways

It's anxiety
that bothers me the most
tight throat, tight head
churning stomach
stew of thoughts

Usually over nothing!

Fortunately
I've
learned
stuff

It's just a matter of remembering
what I've learned

What is it that connects this
moment to the lesson learned?
What lasso, platform of grace   →

makes those neurons connect?

What I've learned:
Self-soothing through music, art and writing
conversation, prayer

Self-soothing through putting oneself
in better situations

Taking care of what one
consumes

Handling what one
should handle...

How an animal suns itself,
breathing, just being itself...
turtle on a log

Cats self-soothe,
they purr if need be
jump start thrums
of happiness

Self-soothe,
smile, have a warm drink,
a bath, hug yourself

Self-soothing
can involve two:
get yourself by
your companion or
family member or friend
and soak up a hug   →

Develop new habits—
Soothe until you don't
even realize you are doing
preventative maintenance

Why even call it self-soothing—
maybe it's just taking care
of yourself—the stuff
of love for yourself!

Love yourself!

— October 22, 2013

PEOPLE ARE LAUGHING IN DELIGHT ALL OVER THE WORLD

It's 4:30 a.m. and people are laughing in delight all over the world. Some get up really early and exercise together, so even here in the U.S. at 4:30 a.m. people are laughing.

It's prime time for office tea and coffee gathering in London. 5.2 million work there, and probably 3.5 million are in offices. At least 5% of these are taking a break right now, and half of that talking, and half again laughing. 43,750 people in London offices are laughing, more or less, right now.

And there are people not in offices... and people all over the world still to consider. If a quarter of us have a decent laugh at least once daily over, say, a 5 minute period, there's a .34% chance that any of us have been laughing in the past five minutes. Multiply that by 7.1 billion people, and 24.1 million of us are laughing, more or less, all over the world. So much delight is being had, and that's good.

— October 23, 2013

LEARNING TO SWIM
for Grandpa Ireland

All the important stuff that happened—
your birth in a toilet bowl as Reality said,
"Get to business, Thurm, swim!"

The seriousness
of losing your mom
who you couldn't remember,
of not being cared for well by your dad
and stepmom, the loving arm relief
you found in grandparents

And the jobs you had as a teen

You drove Grandma in a coal truck
to the prom, attracted her by
decorating your Model A
with polka dots

Billowing signposts that
should be marked by heralds
birds holding words on
floating ribbons unfurling
into filigree wallpaper scene

You and Grandma atop an elopement cake
the amazingness you had children—
were you amazed? And then all the
policies you adeptly enacted for them—
the children, the adopted children
and the cousins taken in—
folding napkins for this one
putting silverware in order for another
steamy comforting clatter from
warm yellow lit kitchen crescendo-ing →

Lady

clashing pans cymbals
pacing domestic scene

Not enough room for all the family?
You built your own house, and
added on additions

Ideas that came via some kind of
hard work and grace to help your hep
with coworkers, bosses, underlings—
"How to Use Humor to Help the Team"

Learn lesson, apply knowledge
when necessary

Daily reports to bosses on a typewriter
written with amusement, the intelligence
of the clatter and splash of type...

You dropped out of high school
and got your education via the font of
civilization—the Cleveland Plain Dealer—
and experience

Cognitive therapy for family members
via example of your memoir—
typesetting the nuts and bolts of it

You wrote about your mistakes
(few though they were)
that would make you
smoke a cigarette in shame—
but this was good, Grandpa
and I left the burrs in,
the things we wouldn't say now

Lady

because Mind has progressed
in some ways

I want people to know
have them see light through thicket
know good though the rough

The polishing of your promise
the possibilities for anyone,
everyone and all

— October 24, 2013

MANY FIBERS GO INTO THIS BUNDLE

Of what I am,
determination scooting
through goo, bootstrap,
ready for more improvement,
making use of that already made

Sculpture hacked from slack,
repeat lessons applied

Water shaping channel for a river,
channel shaping where the water goes

This is where I want to go
I tell the river, this is the channel
we're making—I'm a load on a raft

Or maybe I'm not raft but river,
channeled flood bundled through
strictures I've structured,
forms Mind's accustomed to
or's built with purpose

Maybe I'm the channel
and river is the moment
I'm to put through it

Maybe I'm the river and
the load, channel and
Mind—eye and Mind

Maybe I'm observer,
awake, and Mind
weaves the ride

— October 25, 2013

Lady

BITCHES BREW TRIBUTE NIGHT

A house in a tornado of sound
A spaceship heft with music

Imagine you were hammering
on that house for the first time, hammering
in the basement, on the roof, Thor finding roof
with your hammer, all anti-gravity, finding where
the shingles go, floating loose with your steering wheel ear

Could you imagine if you were
the architect and the carpenter and got to hold
that fucking hammer

What if you were holding
that fucking hammer on your spaceship,
Miles above Earth, banging out the orbit,
inventing the most important work
in the Universe

— *October 26, 2013*

NUTRITION

Healing
from our nucleii
the buds of germs
that heft us

Or not healing per se
but maintenance—
maintaining... better

Being vibrant
plumes of telomeres
long zippers
zipping
and unzipping
as constituent parts
replenish our fabrics,
our waters
our frames

Nucleii kernels of our cells
our cells workers

Smooth chain grain
assembly flow

Productivity
in the body

Mind contributing
minding our body well
mending & maintaining

Pleasing, growing
organizing

Sips of water
purifying, fueling,
replenishing

Much nutrition,
carbs for quick fuel
or long complex ones
for extracted sessions
steady unloading
long capacitance
energizing
the blood

Protein from plants
strong nut magic
strong legume magic
helping our muscles
rebound from tears

Tearing and
subsequent mending
making us stronger

(Work them muscles—
body's there to be used)

Plant fats
avocado, olive
more again
from nuts, too

Fats carrier waves
for vitamin, mineral
absorption   →

All these kernels, germs
eggs of plants
aiding our existence

Nutrition—
a music folding
more wisely
into itself

Better reclamation,
happy fabric for tilling,
fertilizing, recycling,
reuse

— *October 27, 2013*

WILD AND CIVILIZED

Being wild can be
being, civilized
or at least
appreciating
the wild
can be being,
civilized

Young Father—native son—
running out of the bushes
to thrill his little kids
full of ideas

Mom doing stuff
in the tent

Parting leaf
in the dream
that is Reality

I look at young men
younger than me, now
and think about my fertility—
still here—and how I am childless
except I claim
godmotherhood
on everyone,
my solace

Especially the bees—
they are my children

Young men with limbs
thriving,
no wrinkles

→

Lady

or wrinkles
just beginning
to crinkle their leather

Young men pushing strollers—
not only the affluent

I wonder what everyone's
lives are like

Young men I find at farmers markets,
environmental events—

who were their parents?

What is it that got them here,
then, thank goodness

I see these young men
as examples of good
that can be witnessed
when men are not scorned

Young apple maidens
at the tables
in their neo-hippie prints
and/or pencil intellectuals
from universities, again,
at our community events
with shovels and
smart phones

Towheaded children
at the pow wows
hand in hand   →

with dark haired ones
learning about
honoring ancestors
the potential
for revitalization

Civilization
that helps
us find wild

You know me,
America?

I am your native daughter
I am your native son
I am you

— *October 28, 2013*

ELF LADY

Peeling back the avalanche
the headache
the blizzard
the overflowing inbox
the incidents of the nuts & bolts
of dealing with life—
all those card hands

I'm putting all those card hands
in file drawers in their various positions
paperclipped in place
so I can come back to them later,
refreshed, so I can
deal
with what's been dealt better
more gently with myself
yet just kinda crunch
through it
or even let my fellow elves
go to work on it

(I am part elf)

When those cards are filed
or even just left in place
on the table
or left to compost
for the other elves to turn

I'm getting replenished
I'm getting nourishment
I'm getting energy
I'm getting relief

I'm going to church

I'm going to meditate
I'm going to eat
good food
I'm going to
train my legs
on the trail

I'm growing more trees
on the watershed of
me
to harbor life,
livelihood
keep stock

alive

The elves are sitting back
relaxed, too, after their workday

We're investing
in ourselves
We're doing things
in the present
that we are to do
to value the now
and the future,
me & the elves

— October 29, 2013

TO BE TRUE HUMAN

I will
prophesize
and I encourage you
to do so, too
but wait...
before you do it

Let's think about what we want
to see
& let's prophesize
that...

I prophesize
blooms
flowers springing open
gentle velvet unfolding
sproinging normal seasons
budding ad infinitum
until the sun's old age
consumes
this planet

I prophesize the return
of robust populations of bees
tending zest
from pistil to stamen
love nuggets
pollen accreting on
hairy working legs

I prophesize
restoration of habitat, species—
curating every grain and drop
via mind, lab, hand, even nanobot
connecting communities of roaming

fish, fowl, ruminant corridors ensured
wide open plains, too
deserts turned to prairie
fertilized to forest footfall
wolves making more tall growing
trimming just enough deer

I prophesize
awareness
educated holds
securing true truth
the aggregate eye unblinding

Empire will have to get dressed
saying will have to say what it
purports to be and be that—

The competition of the ego,
the striving to be seen best
transforming baser nature
to cooperation
relief, rest, all of us
heaved atop the true top:
the infinite plateau
for the most successful,
which is, innately,
for the gentlest

— *October 30, 2013*

TALKING WITH THE ANCESTORS

Today is Samhain, the ancient Irish holiday
in which fairy folk (I'm part fairy)
and "dead" kin can connect
even more readily
with the living

Honoring relationships & valuing Reality
is what it's about, as are most
holidays

I'm Lady
so I'm compelled
to do stuff for Reality,
help it work stuff out

I welcome this holiday to celebrate the harvest,
note the hastened shortening of daylight,
bundling up of consciousness into
more introspection, the kitchen rituals
of domestic life

And of course this holiday is
for honoring ancestors who are
no longer in the flesh as
we
commonly know it,
here

I address Grandma & Grandpa Ireland
every day in my morning letter
to the Universe

And they talk to me through the radio
of sound & signal that abounds around us →

They give advice, say hello—mostly say hello
& don't worry, be cheerful, & Grandpa says,
"Hey, when are you going to work on
my memoir again?"

I ask them about Heaven, God
oft get some answer about Energy & Christ,
Buddha & Hindu mantras, Universal Mother
& a panoply of references,
spiritual smorgasbord

Lots about Energy
& lots of "I love yous"

(God is pretty OK)

— *October 31, 2013*

Chernin

Writing a poem every day in the month of October 2013 was a challenge for me, both because it was an unusually busy month and because I am not a prolific writer. It's not unusual for me to make multiple revisions in a poem or to spend a day or more sweating over one word. Not having the luxury of that much time led to some different writing for me, which I found interesting. And then, true to my nature, once October was over, I spent the next several months rewriting the poems that interested me most. Those that didn't interest me as much I either left as written or pared down to a few essential lines. As a group, these poems are a sort of diary for the month. I like having that. Thank you for inviting me to participate, John.

— *Shelley Chernin*

Rabbit Rabbit Rabbit

None of us slept the night of September 30th.
Perhaps the shortness of the month. The next day,
we are all so tired. Some jet-lagged, too.
Autumn travels. Leaves flutter past like taunts.

We want to fall, too, but there's no escaping
the Android apps. I survey the venue, balance books,
post Priority mail, meet in person the stockbroker
I'd only ever spoken to over the phone,

until today. After peach green tea, I finish
staff schedules, realize our potential happiness
tranquilizes, pinch my thighs, drive Betty
to the allergist, and eat something. Finally,

the sun releases me. The air cools. Our embrace,
exhausted. Parting kiss, mere precondition for bed.

— *Oct. 1, 2013*

Creeping Charlie

I brush away mown grass,
but let weeds overgrow your slab.
If tickled by leaves,
you hold your laughter.

— Oct. 2, 2013

Shelley Chernin

Poem Superfluous

terzanelle of tongues
body ballad
flesh tercet
finger roundels &
rondeaus & rondelets

his pantoum eyes
& smiles bestow sonnets

— *Oct. 3, 2013*

On the Eve of My 40 Year High School Reunion

Hiking amidst trees here long before
we graduated. Local species—
oak, elm, birch, pine, maple.

Ohio, early October,
needles and leaves, yellowing greens,
browning reds. Like this wood,

we enter autumn in life's confusion
of changing hues. Perhaps, come winter,
through bare branches, we will see.

— *Oct. 4, 2013*

Shelley Chernin

How to Plan a High School Reunion (Part 1)

You will never get started
if you don't vastly underestimate
the amount of your time
that the planning will take.
This is crucial. Make a serious effort
to underestimate dramatically.

Once you've started....

— *Oct. 5, 2013*

How to Plan a High School Reunion (Part 2)

....realize that there isn't time
to write a poem a day
when 200 people depend
upon your ability to plan,
sigh, and....

when at last the reunion is over
postpone the cleanup
to hike in the wood, the day
too hot for October. Savor

the crispy brown topping
on the trail, fallen leaves
like sugared cornflakes
on sweet lokshen kugel.

— Oct. 6, 2013

Light in October

This reminds me of when I was in college and thought that I could write like Faulkner if I drank. I bought a bottle of Jack Daniels or maybe someone bought if for me because I was underage, honestly, I don't know how I managed to get that bottle, but I always had one around somehow, and so,

on this occasion, a Sunday morning because I had no classes, after breakfast in the dorm cafeteria where I probably just had orange juice and cereal, but may have eaten greasy scrambled eggs with buttered toast, as if I could remember a mundane meal that I ate 40 years ago or that the content of the meal even mattered (especially since it stayed down after I went back to my dorm room, which in retrospect was a miracle of sorts),

I pulled out my portable electric typewriter, rolled a sheet of paper into it, opened the bottle of Jack, poured myself a drink, and attempted to write a short story as I downed one, two, maybe three (but I'd be lying if I said I remembered) shots. The sound was the futile click clack of insincere keys. The fury, a girl benumbed and devoiced. Before an hour passed, the drink sent me to nap with nothing typed worth keeping.

A glass of Cabernet tonight while I try to force a poem out onto my computer screen reminds me of that forced attempt to write like Faulkner, to write anything worth keeping. Time to sleep.

— Oct. 7, 2013

I Diverge

Vaporous to dwell
in the clouds,
but we check
and find ground
under feet
we can't feel.

— Oct. 8, 2013

Missing the Port

Milton's sleep broke with the lurch and crunch. He would die in less than three hours, but in the moment of waking, he was annoyed to be disturbed. He'd fed the fish with the Oysters à la Russe, rancid despite the "r" in April. Sleep had been such a relief. He shut his eyes to look for the blue cat that sang "Ave Maria" in his dream. The ship so noisy, with the orchestra playing Berlin's "Everybody's Doing It Now," and that squeaky grinding moan and all the stomping and running above. Must be a wild party. Charles hadn't returned to the cabin yet. He was probably enjoying a glass of Vinho do Porto and a Bock's Rothschild cigar.

Milton realized his thoughts were mere tips of icebergs. He climbed down from the berth, opened his trunk and found the Ohropax tin. He removed two of the wax balls, stuck one in each ear and rejoined the operatic cat. Peace. When the ship snapped in two and the stern went vertical, Milton hurled against the wall without awakening, popping the left earplug loose and fracturing his skull. Ruddy-hued fluid, like pale old tawny, wet his left cheek as freezing water surged in and his heart seized.

— Oct. 9, 2013

How to Open a Jammed Drawer

For breakfast, you offer monogamy. Hungry
past caring whose flapjacks you eat. Smear
on another woman's hot cake. My affect's a
turning, flat. Lift and flip her. I feel nothing
toward the hot griddle—
my lack of jealousy yours not to taste—
your syrup-coated tongue. Sweet love
binds like gluten in the batter, whisk
until moist. Leave lumps. Ladle. Heat. Shallow
bubbles; they'll burst when it's time to tend
our pancakes' browning undersides

I slide
your frosting
spatula
inside and move
the stuff around
or extend
a sturdy wire
carefully
to poke at
stuck things
unseen.

— Oct. 10, 2013

Shelley Chernin

Cyn-Sere

the dog who was afraid
of his master
was the first successful rehydrate

withered bitches littered the gutters
serenely desiccated hopefuls
waiting for hydrant runoff

— *Oct. 11, 2013*

Autumn turns Leda
toward the stars. Stones on her chest
resist Cygnus' pull.

— *Oct. 12, 2013*

Pants Day: May, 1970

Student Handbook:
For girls, dresses and skirts
no shorter than 6 inches above the knee.
No pants.
For boys, whatever they hell they wanted
is how it seemed to us girls.

So here's the plan:
Next Friday, all the girls
wear pants to school.
They can't send us all home.

Friday morning, bus stop:
I'm hip in my groovy purple
plaid pants. Fifteen and bitchin'.
And hedging 'cuz over the pants,
a matching mini overskirt.
Fuck them, if my brother can
wear pants to school,
so can I. Never more confident,
I board the No. 53 bus.
The only girl in pants.

Homeroom:
For about 30 seconds.

After homeroom:
Six girls in the office,
five waiting for their mothers
to bring them skirts.
Me, all I had to do
was remove my pants.
Mini overskirt.
The dress code didn't change that year.

— Oct. 13, 2013

Shelley Chernin

Memories of Poetry at St. Paul's

For Linda Tuthill

This matter of our space
space in all aspects—
a many-windowed room
old glass slightly distorting
the tumble of maple leaves
clock chiming at random

intervals unrelated to the time
that feeling in the chest cavity
of whitespace or shadows
busy with the scurrying
of the nearly manifest
unknown something

something like words shared
to fill the gap in the text of days
closing the distance
between our many hearts
in the space held open for us
by one heart

— Oct. 14, 2013

Shelley Chernin

Today's Stupid List

A university graduate program that requires all applicants to take the GRE but doesn't consider the scores in making admissions decisions. Cost: $185

The famous talk show host (ok, since you insist, it's Oprah) who "corrects" a self-described atheist interviewee by informing her that despite her self-description, the interviewee isn't really an atheist because she feels awe. Cost: TV audience intelligence

A roommate who leaves the apartment knowing that the lock is broken and that his other roommates, who will return before he does, will not be able to get in. Cost: An hour sitting on the stoop

A government that's able to pay its debts but chooses to be on the brink of financial default. Cost: Countless votes

Voters who elected government officials who would opt to default on debts they are able to pay. Cost: Countless lives

— Oct. 15, 2013

Shelley Chernin

Sweet and Spicy Day

Today has rolled onto its left side,
curled up to sleep in the scents
of father oak and a departed witch
hazel lover's uncurled yellow flowers.

— *Oct. 16, 2013*

Oxymoron: Success in the field of poetry.

— Oct. 17, 2013

Shake It Shake It (or Working Late in My Home Office)

In the belly of demand
I'm half the way to dying
hear my heart beat beat in mean time
with its tedious commands:

Eat your spinach. Wash the dishes.
Work until your head goes hazy.
Don't put butter on the self-inflicted
wax burns on your hand.

I might fight my way to freedom
if Outkast's *Hey Ya!* was playing
I might wrest myself from Sing Sing
if the music wasn't canned

but drum machine hypocrisy
like peristaltic waves propels
me through kismetic acids
disassembles my élan

so I'll eat bland obligations
at a work desk piled with answers
tangy questions rot with egg shells
in the kitchen garbage can.

— Oct. 18, 2013

What He Took to His Grave

The $129 two-button suit he bought for weddings and funerals
32 secrets
His laptop password
A white cotton thrift store dress shirt, hidden under which,
his carved ox bone Maori Koru pendant on a hemp cord
All possibility of sleep
A photo of Molly, Bear and Ginger from Christmas 2008
His Jerry Garcia "Emerging Elephant" silk tie
The love of nine women
The unit number of his 10 x10 drive-up self-storage space
Chronic disquiet
Black cap-toe oxfords
His cobweb prison tat
A pair of nylon socks with reinforced toes
His wedding band
Hope that he would ever be known
The dream of a note slipped under his door

— Oct. 19, 2013

Celebrate

The stroke victim who hasn't spoken
in months finds the tongue to say,
"Howard Johnson's fried clams."

— Oct. 20, 2013

Viscosity

write a haiku about my slime he suggests

then a field mouse dies
in my kitchen – unbloodied
soundless – but I scream

— Oct. 21, 2013

Pointillism

I have lost the point
of eye and mind
in small tasks. Dots
hide in the ink
of civil practice
legal form books
and in the shower
grout. I balance
accounts adroitly—
work the zeros,
focus on holey spots—
step back to see
that nothing artful
comes together
without colors.

— Oct. 22, 2013

The Wait

Next year half.
Never catch up.

Increasing fractions
add weight to the bones
of a phantom limb.

— Oct. 23, 2013

you do not understand

you would not love me more
if my writing was accessible

there's lobster bisque in the two-handled Wedgewood cups
and a cross-gabled roof on the children's wing

— *Oct. 24, 2013*

October Snow

engorged on warm lake water
fat wads plop on oak's leafy couch
snap its branchy legs

— Oct. 25, 2013

In the wild hope of paradise
I look out my window into night.
A dog barks once or twice.

— Oct. 26, 2013

Evening Out

lou reed
crosses avenue D
a bit of magic in everything

— Oct. 27, 2013

Unconditional Love Is Crappie

Fried or blackened, it's a game
fish. Take the bait or wait
with bated breath
to be hooked. Gills will be
useless in the pan.

I prefer my love
lemon-grilled, dependent
on hot coals, chef skills
and my vagus nerve.

— *Oct. 28, 2013*

Gold Rush

    1

forty-niners flocked
American River damned
takes hydraulicking

    2

take a small bite, babe,
of an apple tart and hard
like me and your cock

    3

my moon-filled eyes hope
flugelhorns blow the children
to sunny rock homes

— Oct. 29, 2013

Dontcha Wish

the steps to creative richness
                                  were in the head tilt
ten degrees left for pretty words
                                      further to the right for tunes
            just pin down the positions
find direction
                          and angle to amplify the pain
    or capture the clatter
                        of leaves falling from the maple

— Oct. 30, 2013

Shelley Chernin

Tibbar Tibbar Tibbar

Did we fail to conjure the month's rabbit luck?
We cannot know. Legal incantations stole our sleep.
Another childless Halloween, I shower, mail our rent check
at a post office protected by plywood sheets. Then,

the dentist. I leave her office with a face more handsome,
Frankenstein teeth erased by periapical x-ray machine burnout.
Down the road, Thurston the Magician wrangles a red devil
wind's desire to possess the Piasano's Pizza banner. In the car,

dinner's aroma is cheap and easy. Dark early. We're too tired
to light the porch for six-foot trick-or-treaters, although
we crafted their suspenders from ironing board clips.
Let them call us Neanderthals. We are not

their concession stand girls. I am afraid this rain will fell
trees onto our home. Afraid to reverse lucky words.

— Oct. 31, 2013

Shelley Chernin

Burroughs

I had a hell of a time writing a poem a day in October. I had a hard time writing throughout 2013. I spent the first several months of the year going back and forth to Mom, Elyria, her doctors, her hospital bed, her funeral. I spent the next several months unmoored, driving around with the top down, with a new chapbook out of what felt like ancient poems, trying to piece things together. I had a lot of catching up to do with the press (still do), lots of stuff I didn't want to do but needed to, lots more questions than answers, and not much inclination or ability to write. A late night Snoetry rant and two senryu written at Mom's bedside were all the poems I'd written since 2012. As October '13 approached, I felt I had a lot to say, though I wasn't sure what it was or how to say it. I saw people writing every day on Facebook and in the *February 03* book and I thought I could use the discipline. I thought in the process something worthwhile would come out. But I also had a new grandson with serious medical needs, a new job/school opportunity that often kept me busy over twelve hours a day, and a ton of other people's books I'd committed to publishing. So it was hard to keep writing, or even find time to write. Sometimes I had to make myself. And I kept waffling about whether to include my poems in this book. I could've used the "I don't want to self publish" excuse to exclude myself if I found that most of my poems were too execrable. But even at its worst my section is an honest document of my month. It feels like a collection of unvarnished selfies taken at awkward moments. Sometimes my lens is dirty. Sometimes that's on purpose.

— *John Burroughs, 2014.08.01*

Oct. Dawn

You looked far
too warm to have
a cold tonight

And when you
coughed during
my second poem

I wished your
phlegm all over
my body of work

— 2013.10.01

Pitching a Wake

cramped in
culinary math class

my eyes narrow
their stance
plates about
to be crossed

my memory swings
at words I heard
Dave Burba toss
years ago

add them up
connect with
my mantra

"I'll sleep when I'm dead"

— 2013.10.02

Hungry in Cleveland

after a day of restaurant learning
at Edwins on Shaker Square
trying to put the I in chef

this would be chief is home
waiting for the wild card Indians
to start cooking

— 2013.10.03

Fuck It

This is day four
of me writing poems
in homage to a ten
year old book I
still have not read

Enough foreplay

Tonight
I'm taking her
four poets
to bed

— 2013.10.04

Words Dance

at a bowling
alley slash
bar slash
concert venue
in Lakewood
unpinning Ohio
from the gut
a rousing hour
street and not
*con*tent to sit
and spin

here poets
with balls
strike out
cut the dross
unsparing
in winning
form to animate
the long prosaic
and Erie

— *2013.10.05*

Training Camp

My head hurts like a tear
in the fabric of my brain
like a locomotive hit it
at 80 miles per hour
like it's been
waterboarded by
the C.I.A. in an
undisclosed location
and it's all my fault

See I ate a hole
in my own heart
with half a dozen
mason jars of Green
Flash and it all
bled together

Again and again I lie
or dance on the rails
unattractive
waiting
for a cut in
half a chance
with my community
chest yearning
to be smashed
by enough Night Train
or be torn wide
with the untrained scythe
of my presumed immortality

Put me on my back
immobilize me

John Burroughs

cover my face with a shroud
and pour another round

— *2013.10.06*

Need Not

It need not be factual
as long as it's true

It need not be me
if it's you

It need not be my best work
just a snapshot of today

I don't look my finest
every moment anyway

I will write it as I can though
it might not first make sense

Then I'll dig into it later
try to unearth truths not meant

I will pour it out and watch it strive
to breathe and need to writhe

So I'll have something
some poetic prude can criticize

— 2013.10.07

What's Left?

Today the doctor
　　confirmed my fears
　were right after all

I'm losing clarity
　　of vision and will
　require eyeglasses

So that explains
　　why I can't see
　to write today
's poem

— *2013.10.08*

Bubbly

After a week and a half
of classes in culinary math
French cuisine and ServSafe
we move on to cocktail glasses
assorted ales and fine wines
méthode champenoise
and our morale rises

What a gas!

— 2013.10.09

Ink Welling

        All my
        recent
        poems
        seem
        to be
        about
        wanting
       to write 'r
        wanting
        to dip
this pen is   a long shaft
 I plunge   head first

— 2013.10.10

Makes Her Mark

It took a while
for my knee to
attract yours
but when it did
the whole room
seemed to cream
and pulsate
turn reprobate
stiffen in well
lubricated laughter
raw and rhapsodic
as we bohemians
felt the downy heat
of our bourbon
Queen

— 2013.10.11

Blank Et

— 2013.10.12

Reggie Bush in Cleveland

I am Lion.

Here me.

Roar!

— 2013.10.13

Three Sum

You say
I want you
to show me
around town

I only hear
up to you

— 2013.10.14

lamb Knot

Foot fob fall out
Moot mob mall out
Coot cob call out
The bobber of civility

Devil dog dug out
Level log lug out
Bevel bog bug out
The robber of reptility

Better beat ballout
Wetter wheat wallout
Fetter feet fall out
The meter of mobility

— 2013.10.15

Hell In

Today I learned you
have congestive heart
failure

My heart merely aches

— *2013.10.16*

Rough Morning

Snoop Dogg
showed up
for the poetry reading

Before I could
snap his photo
my dog
woke me

— 2013.10.17

Going Garbanzo

It's a full moon
the eve of Sweetest Day
which this year is also
the 20-year anniversary
of my incarceration
and I come home
after ten hours of work
with a neckache to
find five screaming kids
three cacophonous adults
playing a television
a computer game
a Kindle game plus
somebody pissed
on the new couch
and I find you broke
hard promises
leaving me feeling
soiled as I go to
bed with a book
coincidentally
called *A History
of Chickpeas*.

— 2013.10.18

Near Black Jack

Twenty years ago
today I was sent to prison
for eleven years and
I used to have a face
card to go with the time
but now I have only
a *nein* and I feel as out
of place as a German
number ought on a French
record or the menu of
les desserts I'm trying
to learn so I turn up Dead
Kennedys and think
I'll start a Forest Fire
or Riot but keep returning
to their cover of Johnny
Paycheck's Take This Job
and Shove It because
I'd rather publish Dick
Kostelanetz' work in
a condom binding or ogle
Facebook chap crotch selfies
but instead we fight for twenty
years of reasons and one
immediate probable cause
involving babysitting and
an opening I need an excuse
to attend although I drink
too much to drive and sit
in my room writing a whiney
ramble I can't publish while
fantasizing about dogs
taking care of their own
toilet needs because no
matter what anyone says
and no matter how well

→

I learn to make you crème
brûlée or maybe a Napoleon
to me this day will
never be Sweetest.

— 2013.10.19

Slo Brr

Words tear from my
shower curtain like
a lawn mower
in an Arkansas
snow

Dreams scare from my
stower tartan like
a prawn blower
in an Alaskan
know

I've no poems
but plenty of drivel

— 2013.10.20

Po-Poetry

I thought I was out
of poems and sat down
in Dewey's with a cup
of ivory mocha to
contemplate how to break
it to my co-authors

when a cop came in
pointed at the ceramic
elephant tip jar
and said, "I told you
you need to get a pig.
I'll even double your tips
if you put a sign on it
that says Feed the Pig."

We laughed and he said, "Hey
I do all the stereotypical
things police officers do.
I even eat donuts."
Then he took his coffee
and walked out giving
us a final exhortation:
"Maybe you can
find a pig on eBay."

I grunted
pleased
and finally
copped
a poem.

— 2013.10.21

De-Carton

hastain
out rings
what would
box xyr in

to miss pique
say has stain
or limit by
pronoun
might reveal
a vision gap
or dirty need
to punch holes
without consent

think about it

let beauty be
indelible

love being
stop boxing

— 2013.10.22

Bon Appétit

At the restaurant
most our eight
year anniversary

See we eight
our marriage
before it ate us

— 2013.10.23

Po' 'Em

(for Bill Beers, West Geauga School Board President, who has a "performance index scores" fetish, during his reelection campaign)

The electorate is drinking
Our schools are sinking

For sake of education
Three cheers for Beers

— 2013.10.24

Y in Tasting

Brandon gets pouring

Recommends we spit
(class before work)

I say yes
and I must

Swallow

— 2013.10.25

Soft Opening

Drag
myself out
red wine
lobster bisque
red wine
mixed field greens
ice water
French bread
braised rabbit
sweet potato purée
down my shirt
best I've had
more water
chocolate duo
Scotch ale
listless no more

— 2013.10.26

Dead

Lou Reed's liver
finally had enough

— 2013.10.27

Priorities

The night Lou Reed died
I lay in bed and wrote
an epic poem in my head

Then I fell asleep
dreamt of dear dead Mom
and forgot it

— 2013.10.28

Cheating

The night Lou Reed died
I recommitted to writing
a poem a day

But I have problems
with commitment

— 2013.10.29   [really written on 10.30]

Muddle Fruit

What passion
fruit becomes
after marriage

— 2013.10.30

Fine

All's well
that ends

— *2013.10.31*

Brightman

Shybtman

I didn't really have a pre-set approach to October. No more than I normally do: what about that particular day caught most my attention? This is my catalog, this is my codex, this is my confession.

— *Steve Brightman*

Something With Edges

With a cheesecloth
over his eyes,
he feels dumbly
for something with edges.
That way he knows
he's not adrift.
This way he knows
he's still connected,
even if that makes him
the Hindenburg.

— 1 October 2013

The Gun That Isn't A Gun

My face is the faceless.
Your face is the faceless.
Bones by the thousands
are growing weaker under
the gun that isn't a gun,
but is used to take hostage.
Lungs fill to half capacity
in the shadow of this day.
You do not need your breath.
You do not need your health.
May your heart not collude
with your last of nights
until absolutely necessary.
You will need it to stay strong.
You will need it to continue
to clench and unclench.

— 2 October 2013

It's Changing

It's changing.
It's changing not.
There is no stasis today.
It's changing.
It's changing not.
Each of your poems,
platonic or romantic;
each of your kisses,
platonic or romantic;
each of your griefs,
platonic or romantic
are changing the world.
It's changing.
It's changing not.
You are microscopic and
you are majestic.
It's changing.
It's changing not.
You are not dragon
or downward dog.
You are one tinny voice
against a cascade.
It's changing.
It's changing not.
You are not static today.
You are crashing wave.
You are falling petals.
You are.

— 3 October 2013

Down To Here

Trace my finger
across vapor trails
when the moon
ain't due for hours.

No time to wait
for rainbows in
a cloud free sky.

Slowly unzip
the atmosphere,
drag the heavens
down to here.

Trace my finger
across Fortuna's spine
when Diana
isn't due for hours.

— 4 October 2013

Going Door To Door

Woke up
this morning to
a blanket of
Saturday cool
and a black spot
on the sun.

It could be
dark omen,
it could be
bulk mail from
mostly uninterested
angels.

They're bored to
heavenly tears with
going door to door
so they've pooled
their remaining assets
and propped up
the US Postal Service
until they've got their
website up and running.

— 5 October 2013

Colour By Numbers

I stumble into
this blank canvas
with my swollen
paintbrush tongue
filling in the gaps
like I was born
for nothing else.

— 6 October 2013

Driving Days

The day I knew
she was my native tongue
was a day she didn't
say anything at all.
It was driving day —
a good majority of our days
are driving days —
and we were heading south,
away from the lake.
We took one of those
cloverleaf off-ramps
and she shifted
her left leg to the door
ahead of the curve.
This was how she told me
that she thought it was
the wrong direction.
Her knee dipped into
the warmth of silence
and resurfaced as
compound word,
one with no literal
translation.

— 7 October 2013

To Welcome Them

This is a night,
like some others
in my past,
where the words
come as they are;
guests who are
as unfamiliar with me
as I am with them.
I do my best to
accommodate
their travels and want
to welcome them.
I set a table
by the door with
bread and salt,
hoping that they
will make themselves
at home.

— 8 October 2013

Warm Comfort Now

Warm comfort now
in perfect straight pew.
sunlight and seven seas
on this the eve
of the tenth day of
the tenth month.
Warm comfort now
in crooked mile road show.
Butter orange trees
on this the eve
of every last day of
every last month.
warm comfort now
in apology and hallelujah.
rocking chair voices
on this the eve
of unruly heavens
and pitch black
everything.

— 9 October 2013

Foxtrot Foxtrot November Alpha

Speakerphone
hold notes
toggle between
lines one and two.
Every voice
is a command,
every voice
a demand.
Foxtrot.
Foxtrot.
November.
Alpha.
Echo chamber
photographs
better than
your mirror.
All the grey
disappeared.
All the voices
cry all clear.

— *10 October 2013*

Outside Tonight

Voices hold
at gravel pitch,
cover the smother
and the ribs
show through skin.
Outside tonight
the moon is not
the moon, but
is a space station
and we are all small,
we are all ribs
or appendix.
We are all thumbs
and slacked jaws,
dumb apes
with math tricks
and jet fuel.
Voices cannot
hold for much
longer.

— 11 October 2013

His Shirt Was Untucked

The first time I'd saw him was
at the aquarium. I thought he said
that he was on a field trip that day.
Lou Reed remembered my name
the day I saw him a second time.
I wasn't sure it was him, at first,
until he shouted (as much as Lou Reed
would ever need to shout) "Steve."
He was eating ice cream sandwiches
in the shadows of the concourse.
His hair was a mess and his shirt
was untucked, a solid black t-shirt.

— *12 October 2013*

Drop Everything

This journey can never be
measured by rotations
of the earth around the sun
or around its very own axis.
This is something you have to
do while looking time right
in its milky, snarled eye.
You have to find the place
where you first remember dying.
Then you have to drop everything
you think is important and
get your ass back to that spot.
Don't worry about tying up
whatever you think are loose ends.
Loose ends to you are
mooring lines to someone else.
Someone is hanging on
for dear life, not knowing what
they are tethered to today.
Get back to the spot
where you first remember dying.
Then remember how far you've
been since that tiny death.
Remember how many tiny deaths
you've had since then.
Remember that you are
invincible in your vulnerability.
Remember, now, that you
are moored to someone, too,
that you are not mere witness.
You are participant, breathing,
and that this is your journey
and it is not finished.

— *13 October 2013*

Steve Brightman

The Sunset Bigger

Intolerable strain
upon eye apple eye;
that's what hollered
the wooden doctor
from the top step
of his porch that
sloped gently to
the west and into
the sunset bigger
than an apple is
when you hold it
three inches from
the tip of your nose.

— 14 October 2013

Steve Brightman

A Quick Walk To Name Things

Four college kids in sweatshirts
for the first time this semester and

vacancy where there used to be
building and streetcar and gravel;

silo and rail and rotted lumber,
weeds and unidentified fur scurry.

a stoplight is changing from red
to green, back to red from yellow.

— *15 October 2013*

Wild Side

Lou Reed flew into
the city of rust
in one plane, yellowed.
His liver arrived on
another and he
snuck out of there
a transformed fellow,
but not until after
the anesthesiologist said
count backward from
two two two, two, two two two two...

— 16 October 2013

Steve Brightman

Temptation Moon

Lou Reed is
all suspension
and no bridge.
Lou Reed is
dusted pale,
piano androgyny,
temptation moon,
electric alchemy.
Lou Reed is
all suspension
and no disbelief.
Lou Reed is.

— 17 October 2013

A Matter Of Perspective

Tonight,
shortly after
you arrive,
the moon
will pass behind
the earth.
Sun, earth,
and moon
will align and
we will walk
outside into
the backyard and
feel wet grass
beneath our feet
and we will crane
our puny necks.

— 18 October 2013

Still Be There Tomorrow

Today was rain.
And more rain.
It was stay indoors
with soup simmering
until sundown.
It was sugar-dusted
audible, and hours
upon the couch.
It was hear the
mailbox rattling
in the wind and
leaving it be because
it would still be
there tomorrow.
It was ice cream
before dinner
and leaving the
dishes in the sink
overnight.

— 19 October 2013

Impossible To Tell

Psychedelic rust
lunar aftermath
amplified amplified,
and after the
eleventh time,
it becomes
impossible to tell
whether Lou Reed
is saying
Lisa says or
Jesus saves.

— *20 October 2013*

Tucked Safely

Off-kilter
aquamarine;
bare bulb,
throw the
switch,
already.
Myths are born
somewhere,
this one started
where it finished:
tucked safely
at night
into riverbed,
no time for sleep
when arroyos
are bear traps
and sunlight
is your worst
enemy.

— 21 October 2013

Her Fair Share

It was about noon today
when it struck me that
the blank page too often
resembles rushing headlong
into the street without
looking both ways first.
It is an insult to my mother
to leave it there, unattended.
She took her fair share
of sunny afternoons when
Nixon was king teaching me
better than to do that.
I type. I pronounce words
aloud to ensure that they
make sense in the way
that they dodge traffic,
accumulating on the other
side of the street, like
one thousand answers to
the same awful riddle.

— 22 October 2013

Dish Strainer Dry

You do not set
your shoes on the
counter anymore,
even though the
old superstition is
about hats on beds.
You are not concerned
with spots on glassware,
you are convinced that
there is no dry like
dish strainer dry
because the run-off
falls slower than
the eye can see and
slicks the porcelain
while you sleep.

— *23 October 2013*

Steve Brightman

Lingered Long Through The Windows

October into November
is the most precarious
stretch of Ohio calendar;
the drive to work was
an unknowing race against
the blizzard that wasn't
and I almost wanted to
make the evening news
a part of my day, so that
I would know how to dress
the next few mornings.
Weathering the headlines,
however, was enough to
decide against it while
grey lingered long
through the windows
and the couch grew warmer
as every minute passed.

— 24 October 2013

Ugly Obligation

Ugly obligation,
open mouth.
Every word
spoken lost in
translation.
Ugly obligation,
swollen tongue.
Translation
begets new
translation
until every
single voice
has turned
on itself and
looks like a
snake that's
swallowed
its own tail.
Ugly obligation,
choking sounds.

— 25 October 2013

Cross-Legged

I don't remember
the exactness of his face,
but I can still see the
angry hollow of his cheeks
when I cheered for Ali
on Wide World of Sports
while sitting, cross-legged,
in his mother's living room.
I remember just two times
his hand reached for mine.
Once when we shared an
incredible green swell of
pistachio ice cream from
Baskin-Robbins, and the
other in the desert, when
we'd camped atop sand
and fired handguns at
green bottles near sunset.

— 26 October 2013

One Yahoo At Yahoo

It didn't take long
for the world to fall
to its knees
when word came.
Even less time,
it seems,
for parasites and
music reviewers
to spoonfeed
your import to us.
One yahoo at Yahoo
chimed in with
"Listen to 15
of Lou Reed's
Overlooked Gems,"
so I did.
I played all fifteen
at the same time,
a dishonest homage
among obituaries.
I listened to fifteen
chapters of your
great American novel
all at once and there's
nothing that we have
in common, not even
our name.

— 27 October 2013

Asphalt Is For Quitters

Tonight is one more step
along this dirt road song.

Everyone can hear the rhythms
along this dirt road song.

Asphalt is for quitters
along this dirt road song.

Everyone can see the flats
along this dirt road song.

Tonight is one more step
for you and me and the rest to see
along this dirt road song.

Asphalt is for quitters
along this dirt road song.

— 28 October 2013

Sunset To Sunrise

It's been a long damn time
since I've been afraid of that voice,
afraid of the narrator,
afraid of what the dark has
in that big back pocket of hers.
I have forgotten the terrors.
Forgotten the grappling hook
lifeline fingernails into sheer face
of rock, of drywall, of Egyptian cotton,
of the closest damn flat surface.
I have forgotten the bourbon.
Forgotten the psychedelics and
the sunset to sunrise cd spin
listening to the one and only voice.
It wasn't God, but that fucker
had a microphone and amplification
was enough to get me through.
There was harm in her eye.
It's been a long damn time
since I even remembered trying
to get my wiggling fingers
into that big back pocket of hers.
I have forgotten the painted desert,
forgotten the continental divide,
forgotten Lewis, forgotten Clark,
forgotten that my grandfather
was born on a wooden kitchen table
in a farmhouse on the plains
outside of Chicago, born in a
farmhouse that is now a steakhouse
on a frontage road approximately
.2 miles from the freeway
according to Google maps.

— 29 October 2013

Steve Brightman

No Tiny Wisdoms

You wouldn't think
it would be easy to
confuse Confucius
with the ocean;
what with the silence
on all sides once
you get far enough away
from the shoreline.
Yet here we stand,
feet in the sand,
on this the last
Wednesday in October.
He has no tiny wisdoms
for us tonight, only
beaches littered
with starfish
left behind by
the ebb tide.

— 30 October 2013

The Man With The Grey Stubble

Neither ghoul nor goblin
visited my porch today.
Neither superman nor princess
darkened my doorway.
I was not prepared for them,
so it is all for the best.
They would have had a hard time
explaining to their parents
at the end of the drive
why the man with grey stubble
in the blue house
handed out Q-tips or pennies
or unsalted peanuts,
while his parrot screeched
at visitors who were
walking away with his food.

— *31 October 2013*

Acknowledgments

"Pants Day: May, 1970" by Shelley Chernin was first published in *Vending Machine: Poetry for Change, Volume 4* and nominated for a Pushcart Prize by The Poet's Haven.

An early version of "Po-poetry" by John Burroughs was first published in *The City*.

"Words Dance" and "Makes Her Mark" by John Burroughs were first published as limited edition broadsides by 48th Street Press.

"Training Camp" by John Burroughs was first published in the *2014 Hessler Street Fair Poetry Anthology*.

"It's Changing" by Steve Brightman was also first published in *Vending Machine: Poetry for Change, Volume 4*.

"His Shirt Was Untucked," "Wild Side," "Temptation Moon," "Impossible to Tell" and "One Yahoo at Yahoo" by Steve Brightman were first published in his chapbook *13 Ways of Looking at Lou Reed* by Crisis Chronicles Press.

Some poems in this book previously appeared online (sometimes in different versions) either as Facebook notes or on their authors' blogs.

About the Authors

Dr. Mary Weems is a poet, playwright, imagination-intellect theorist, social/cultural foundations scholar and former Poet Laureate of Cleveland Heights. Weems is the author and/or editor of twelve books and five chapbooks, most notably *white* (Wick Poetry Chapbook Series) and *Tampon Class* (Pavement Saw Press). Two of her books were full collections of poetry: *An Unmistakable Shade of Red and the Obama Chronicles* (Bottom Dog Press, 2008) and *For(e)closure* (Main Street Rag Press, 2012), both finalists for Ohioana Book awards.

John Swain of Louisville, Kentucky, is the author of several acclaimed books including *Rain and Gravestones* (2013, Crisis Chronicles), *White Vases* (2012, Crisis Chronicles) and *Prominences* (2011, Flutter Press). His latest, *Ring the Sycamore Sky*, was just released in the summer of 2014 by Red Paint Hill Publishing.

Steven B. Smith was born, is living, will die. He's been a poet 50 years, artist 49 years, the publisher of *ArtCrimes*, editor of AgentOfChaos.com, he blogs on WalkingThinIce.com, and sings at ReverbNation.com/MutantSmith. Smith & Lady published his bio *Stations of the Lost & Found, a True Tale of Armed Robbery, Stolen Cars, Outsider Art, Mutant Poetry, Underground Publishing, Robbing the Cradle, and Leaving the Country* in 2012 via The City Poetry Press.

Lady, a.k.a. Kathy Ireland Smith, is a poet, publisher, artist and surreal photographer from northeast Ohio. She and her husband Smith spent 31 months of traveling in 10 countries on 3 continents from 2006-9, and you can follow their ongoing adventures at WalkingThinIce.com. Kathy is also founder and editor of The City Poetry (thecitypoetry.com), a cutting edge art and poetry zine based in Cleveland.

Shelley Chernin is a freelance researcher, writer and editor of legal reference books and a ukulele enthusiast. Her poems have appeared in places like *Great Lakes Review, Scrivener Creative Review, Rhapsoidia, Durable Goods, Big Bridge*, and the *Heights Observer*. She was awarded 2nd Place in the 2011 Hessler Street Fair Poetry Contest. Her chapbook, *The Vigil*, was published in 2012 by Crisis Chronicles.

Steve Brightman lives in Kent, Ohio. He firmly believes in two seasons: winter and baseball. His most recent chapbooks include *13 Ways of Looking at Lou Reed* (2013, Crisis Chronicles Press), *In Brilliant Explosions Alone* (2013, NightBallet Press); *Like Michelangelo Sorta Said* (2013, The Poet's Haven), *Absent The* (2013, Writing Knights Press) and *Sometimes, Illinois* (2011, NightBallet).

John Burroughs is the founding editor of Crisis Chronicles Press and hosts the Monday at Mahall's Poetry and Prose Series in Lakewood, Ohio. He is the author of *It Takes More Than Chance to Make Change* (2013, The Poet's Haven), *The Eater of the Absurd* (2012, NightBallet Press), Barry Merry Baloney (2012, Spare Change Press), Water Works (2012, recycled karma press), Electric Company (2011, Writing Knights) and more.

Also from Crisis Chronicles:

CC#108 — *Soul Picked Clean* by Cat Russell
CC#107 — *Our house on the sand* by Elaine Schleiffer
CC#106 — *The Law of Almosts* by Mindi Kirchner
CC#105 — *Triple Threat* by John Dorsey
CC#104 — *Awaiting Time* by Helen Shepard
CC#103 — *Drinking From What I Once Wore: Selected and Recent Poems* by Chris Stroffolino
CC#102 — *Malformed Confetti* by Juliet Cook
CC#101 — *Dodge, Tuck, Roll* by Rikki Santer
CC#100 — *The Strength of Flowers* by Steve Thomas
CC#99 — *Citizen of Metropolis* by Christine Howey
CC#98 — *Where Never Was Already Is* by Steven B. Smith
CC#97 — *Serving* by Kari Gunter-Seymour
CC#96 — *Oct Tongue 2* by Lyn Lifshin, George Wallace, Dianne Borsenik, Eric Anderson, Kathleen Cerveny, Juliet Cook, Mark Sebastian Jordan and Margaret Bashaar
CC#95 — *Hourglass Studies* by Krysia Jopek
CC#94 — *Inquiry into Loneliness* by Meg Harris
CC#93 — *Snap* by Dion Farquhar
CC#92 — *Diary of a Feminist Thug, Volume I: His[tories] of Her Land* by Lyz Bly [co-published with Guide to Kulchur Books]
CC#91 — *Turnstile Burlesque* by John Greiner
CC#90 — *Sandpaper Lovin'* by Victor Clevenger
CC#89 — *The Black Between Stars* by Elliot Nicely
CC#88 — *Scraping the Sky* by Luba Gawur
CC#87 — *13 Poems from the Edge of Extinction* by Adrian Manning
CC#86 — *Bestiary* by Michael Estabrook
CC#85 — *2016 Hessler Street Fair Poetry Anthology* by 100+ poets
CC#84 — *God Save Your Mad Parade* by Austen Roye
CC#83 — *Age of Aquarius: Collected Poems 1981-2016* by Dianne Borsenik
CC#82 — *Ship of Theseus* by Christopher Willard
CC#81 — *Under My Dark* by Lana Bella
CC#80 — *When You Don't Know Who You Are* by Alinda Dickinson Wasner
CC#79 — *Fractured Fairy Tales* by William Merricle
CC#78 — *xx poems* by Jennifer MacBain-Stephens
CC#77 — *Special Watch* by Richard M. O'Donnell
CC#76 — *The Gravity of Chainsaws* by Azriel Johnson
CC#75 — *This Frankenstein Union* by Esteban Colon
CC#74 — *Drink Drank Drunk* by Bradford Middleton
CC#73 — *Contents Under Pressure* by Kevin Ridgeway
CC#72 — *Ghost on the Inside* by John Dorsey
CC#71 — *Readings / The Road: Two Poems from Euclid Creek Book* Three by Michael Ceraolo

CC#70 — *Matilda's Battle Waltz* by Tracie Morell
CC#69 — *2015 Hessler Street Fair Poetry Anthology* by 104 poets
CC#68 — *Balefire* by Susan Sheppard
CC#67 — *Bookmobile: From the Library of Jesus Crisis* by David S. Pointer
CC#66 — *Thunderclap Amen* by Dianne Borsenik
CC#65 — *Cutting the Möbius* by Jonathan Thorn
CC#64 — *Be Closer for My Burn* by Robin Wyatt Dunn
CC#63 — *#ThisIsCLE: An Anthology of the 2014 Best Cleveland Poem Competition* by various authors
CC#62 — *I Don't* by Bree
CC#61 — *HOLDING STORIES in YOUR HANDS: Narrative Poems and Poetic Narratives* by Elise Geither
CC#60 — *The Night Market* by D.R. Wagner
CC#59 — *Ohio Triangle* by Alex Gildzen
CC#58 — *Poems for Explosion* by John G. Hall
CC#57 — *City of Tents: Poems About the Occupy Movement and Other Items Taken From the News* by Martin Willitts, Jr.
CC#56 — *Irises Made of Moth Wings* by Christian O'Keeffe [out of print]
CC#55 — *Oct Tongue -1* by Mary Weems, John Swain, Steven Smith, Lady, Shelley Chernin, John Burroughs and Steve Brightman
CC#54 — *Songs in the Key of Cleveland: An Anthology of the 2013 Best Cleveland Poem Competition* by 12 authors
CC#53 — *Cut Me Free* by Ben Heins [out of print]
CC#52 — *In Bold Blackness: Selections* by Jami Tillis
CC#51 — *Sunshine Liar* by Ryan Swofford [out of print]
CC#50 — *YES, but…* by Martin Burke
CC#49 — *Every Bird, To You* by Sarah Marcus [out of print]
CC#48 — *13 Ways Of Looking At Lou Reed* by Steve Brightman
CC#47 — *secret letters* by j/j hastain
CC#46 — *Cleveland: Point B in Ohio Triangle* by Alex Gildzen [out of print]
CC#45 — *Rain and Gravestones* by John Swain
CC#44 — *Cheap and Easy Magazine, volume 1* by 36 authors/artists
CC#43 — *Bus Riders in the Storm* by Cee Williams
CC#42 — *My America* by Cee Williams
CC#41 — *The Everyday Parade / Alone With Turntable, Old Records* by Justin Hamm [out of print]
CC#40 — *Howl for My Family in April* by Mary C. O'Malley [out of print]
CC#39 — *Body Voices* by Kevin Reid
CC#38 — *the melody, I swear, its just around that way: volume 2* by Bree [out of print]
CC#37 — *Grand Slam* by Alan S. Kleiman
CC#36 — *Red Hibiscus* by Heather Ann Schmidt
CC#35 — *Photograph* by Jackie Koch
CC#34 — *Queen of Dorksville* by Leah Mueller
CC#33 — *Angel* by Sandy Sue Benitez
CC#32 — *In Circles* by Ryn Cricket

CC#31 — *The Other Guy* by John Thomas Allen
CC#30 — *as she unbends* by Jolynne Hudnell
CC#29 — *Street maps for lost souls* by John Dorsey [out of print]
CC#28 — *I Can Live with Death* by David B. McCoy
CC#27 — *The Wandering White* [broadside] by d.a. levy [out of print]
CC#26 — *White Vases* by John Swain
CC#25 — *The Anarchist's Blac Book of Poetry* by Frankie Metro [out of print]
CC#24 — *The Vigil* by Shelley Chernin
CC#23 — *This Is How She Fails* by Lisa J. Cihlar
CC#22 — *desire lines* by Chansonette Buck
CC#21 — *12 Poems* by Cee Williams
CC#20 — *Lens* by John Burroughs, a.k.a. Jesus Crisis [out of print]
CC#19 — *Primer for the Vanguard Youth* by RA Washington
CC#18 — *Only Human by Definition* by Jay Passer
CC#17 — *Rapid Eye Movement* by J.E. Stanley
CC#16 — *Grace, You Let the Screen Door Slam* by William Merricle
CC#15 — *the melody, I swear, its just around that way* by Bree [out of print]
CC#14 — *Burnin' Shadows* by Kevin Eberhardt
CC#13 — *Fracture Mechanics/TRAP DOORS* by Michael Bernstein
CC#12 — *Unruly* by Steven B. Smith [out of print]
CC#11 — *Blue Graffiti* by Dianne Borsenik
CC#10 — *Fever Dreams* by Yahia Lababidi [out of print]
CC#9 — *Transient Angels* by Heather Ann Schmidt
CC#8 — *Identity Crisis* by Jesus Crisis
CC#7 — *Fuck Poetry* anthology by 40 authors [out of print]
CC#6 — *The Bat's Love Song: American Haiku* by Heather Ann Schmidt [out of print]
CC#5 — *Suburban Monastery Death Poem* by d.a. levy
CC#4 — *Elyria: Point A in Ohio Triangle* by Alex Gildzen [out of print]
CC#3 — *6/9 Improvisations in Dependence* by Jesus Crisis [out of print]
CC#2 — *HardDrive/SoftWear* by Dianne Borsenik [out of print]
CC#1 — *Bloggerel* by Jesus Crisis [out of print]

And we have more titles coming soon by Nicole Hennessy, Carolyn Srygley-Moore, Christopher Franke, Lisa Cihlar, Julie Ursem Marchand, Kent Taylor, Alex Gildzen, D. R. Wagner and Chansonette Buck with Jillian Mardin.

To get any Crisis Chronicles title, send ten US dollars to John Burroughs, 3431 George Avenue, Parma, Ohio USA. Or purchase via PayPal to jc@crisischronicles.com. Please add a few dollars for international orders.

www.ingramcontent.com/pod-product-compliance
Lightning Source LLC
Chambersburg PA
CBHW071110160426
43196CB00013B/2524